"Forgiveness as the Pathway: Heali

Forgiveness as t

Healing

the Mind

the Body

the Soul

Sonya D. Smith

"Forgiveness as the Pathway: Healing the Mind the Body the Soul"

Copyright © 2024 Sonya D. Smith

This book was created with the assistance of ChatGPT, an AI language model developed by OpenAI.

Book Cover: MidJourney/Canva

KDP Formatting: @thomas_kindle (Fiverr)

All rights reserved.

"Forgiveness as the Pathway: Healing the Mind the Body the Soul"

DEDICATION

Your strength in vulnerability, your courage in sharing the depths of your hurt, has been the inspiration for every word written in these pages. It was our conversation that day, the profound innerstanding of the pain you have carried, that ignited the spark for this journey into forgiveness. This book is more than just a collection of thoughts and insights; it is a testament to the resilience of your spirit and a hope—a beacon—aiming to guide you towards the path of healing and forgiveness.

May these words serve as a bridge, not just for you but for anyone who has felt the sting of similar wounds, to cross over from the shadows of the past into the light of peace and forgiveness. This is for you, in the hope that you find solace, understanding, and the freedom that forgiveness brings. Your journey has the power to transform not just your own life but the lives of all it touches.

With all my love and unwavering belief in the journey ahead!

"Forgiveness as the Pathway: Healing the Mind the Body the Soul"

"Forgiveness as the Pathway: Healing the Mind the Body the Soul"

CONTENTS

	Acknowledgments	7
1	UNDERSTANDING FORGIVENESS	11
2	THE WOUNDS WITHIN	19
3	THE JOURNEY TO FORGIVENESS	27
4	FORGIVENESS AND HEALING THE MIND	33
5	FORGIVENESS AND HEALING THE BODY	42
6	FORGIVENESS AND HEALING THE SOUL	49
7	LIVING A LIFE OF FORGIVENESS	57
8	TOOLS AND EXERCISES FOR FORGIVENESS	65
	STORIES OF FORGIVENESS	77
	ABOUT THE AUTHOR	79

"Forgiveness as the Pathway: Healing the Mind the Body the Soul"

"Forgiveness as the Pathway: Healing the Mind the Body the Soul"

ACKNOWLEDGMENTS

In crafting this book, my appreciation stretches far and wide, touching the hearts of many who have contributed to its realization in varied and profound ways. Yet, among these cherished contributors, there stands one whose influence resonates at the very core of this journey—a very special loved one. His courage in confronting the shadows of past hurts, and sharing the depth of his pain, has been the profound spark that inspired this exploration into forgiveness. This book is a testament to his strength, and a beacon of hope for all who seek solace and understanding in their own journeys toward healing.

I extend my heartfelt thanks to my mentors, my friends, and the experts who have guided me with their wisdom and insights, enriching this narrative with depth and compassion. To my family, whose unwavering support and love have been my anchor, I am forever appreciative. To the professionals who meticulously shaped and refined this manuscript, your dedication has brought these words to life.

And to YOU embarking on your own paths of forgiveness, this work is shared with you in the spirit of solidarity and hope. May it light your way toward peace and renewal.

Above all, to my special loved one, this book stands as a bridge—built from our shared experiences and conversations—reaching towards understanding, forgiveness, and the profound healing we can find within it. Thank you for being the unwitting muse, the catalyst for a journey that I hope will inspire and heal many.

"Forgiveness as the Pathway: Healing the Mind the Body the Soul"

"Forgiveness as the Pathway: Healing the Mind the Body the Soul"

"Forgiveness is the silent music of the soul that dances away the shadows of our burdens, inviting light to heal the hidden corners of our being."

"Forgiveness as the Pathway: Healing the Mind the Body the Soul"

In the vast expanse of human emotion and experience, forgiveness emerges as a powerful beacon of healing and transformation. "Forgiveness as the Pathway: Healing the Mind, the Body, the Soul" ventures into the heart of this profound act, unraveling its capacity to mend the fractures within your psyche, soothe your physical ailments, and restore the vibrancy of your spirit. This book is not just a narrative but a journey—a passage through the layers of pain, resentment, and hurt towards a destination of peace, health, and spiritual renewal.

At its essence, forgiveness is depicted here as a key, unlocking doors to inner sanctuaries of peace and well-being that many have forgotten or believed permanently sealed. The journey of forgiveness is one of rediscovery, where the landscapes of the mind, body, and soul are navigated with compassion, understanding, and an unwavering commitment to healing. Through the act of forgiving, you confront your vulnerabilities and transform them into strengths, charting a course towards a life of greater fulfillment and harmony.

"Forgiveness as the Pathway: Healing the Mind, the Body, the Soul" invites you to explore forgiveness as a multidimensional process, one that transcends the act of merely letting go of anger and resentment. It delves into the intricacies of human relationships, the burdens of carrying unresolved pain, and the liberation found in forgiveness. By weaving together insights from psychology, spirituality, and real-life stories of transformation, this book illuminates the path to healing and wholeness.

As you journey through its pages, you are encouraged to reflect on your own experiences, to confront the shadows of your past, and to embrace forgiveness as a practice of self-love and self-liberation. This book serves as a guide, offering practical tools and exercises to help you navigate the complex terrain of forgiving and to foster an environment within which healing can flourish.

"Forgiveness as the Pathway: Healing the Mind, the Body, the Soul" is more than just a title; it is a philosophy, a way of living that promotes inner peace, physical health, and spiritual growth. It is an invitation to embark on the most noble of human endeavors—to forgive, not only others but also oneself. In doing so, you unlock the fullest potential of your being, discovering along the way the infinite capacity of the human heart to heal, to love, and to transcend.

1 UNDERSTANDING FORGIVENESS

"Forgiveness is the bridge that connects the shores of hurt and healing, allowing you to cross from the land of pain into the realms of peace and understanding."

At the very outset of your journey through "Forgiveness as the Pathway: Healing the Mind, the Body, the Soul," you find yourself standing at the threshold of understanding—an essential step before you can truly embark on the transformative path of forgiveness. This opening chapter serves as an invitation to delve deeper into the essence of forgiveness, unraveling its complexities and revealing its profound impact on your life.

Forgiveness is often shrouded in misconceptions and myths. It is frequently mistaken for a sign of weakness, a forgetful act, or an instantaneous solution to deep-seated pain. However, true forgiveness is none of these. It is a deliberate, often challenging process that involves a deep understanding of oneself and others. It requires you to confront your pain, acknowledge your hurt, and extend empathy both to yourself and those who have wronged you. This chapter aims to demystify forgiveness, presenting it as a powerful tool for healing and personal growth.

Understanding forgiveness begins with recognizing that it is a choice—a choice that liberates the forgiver more than the forgiven. It is a gift of freedom to oneself, a decision to no longer be defined by the grievances of the past. By choosing forgiveness, you allow yourself to release the burdens of bitterness and resentment, paving the way for peace, happiness, and well-being.

This chapter explores the psychological underpinnings of forgiveness, highlighting how your mind process hurt and the transformative power of altering your perceptions. It examines the emotional journey of forgiveness, from the initial pain and anger to the eventual release and peace. Furthermore, it addresses the spiritual dimensions of forgiveness, suggesting that forgiving is not just an act of reconciliation but a profound spiritual practice that connects you to your innermost self and the essence of humanity.

Through engaging narratives, insightful analysis, and practical advice,

"Forgiveness as the Pathway: Healing the Mind the Body the Soul"

"Understanding Forgiveness" sets the stage for the rest of the book. It encourages you to reflect on your own experiences of forgiveness, to question your long-held beliefs, and to open your heart to the possibilities of healing and renewal. As you traverse this chapter, you learn not only the true meaning of forgiveness but also its indispensable role in your journey towards healing the mind, the body, and the soul.

The true meaning of forgiveness

The true meaning of forgiveness transcends the common perception of it as merely letting go of resentment or offering absolution to someone who has wronged you. At its core, forgiveness is a profound, multi-layered process that involves deep emotional and psychological work, aimed not only at releasing negative feelings but at fostering understanding, compassion, and even love, in the face of hurt and betrayal.

Forgiveness is an act of profound courage and strength. It requires you to face the pain inflicted upon you, whether through betrayal, injustice, or neglect, and to confront the emotions that this pain evokes. It asks you to look beyond your immediate reactions of anger and hurt, to see the situation and the people involved with greater clarity and empathy. This is not to excuse harmful behavior or to deny the validity of your feelings but to understand that holding onto anger and resentment binds you to the past in a way that hampers your own healing and growth.

The true meaning of forgiveness also lies in the recognition that, as humans, we are all fallible. We all make mistakes, act out of ignorance or hurt, and sometimes cause pain to others, intentionally or unintentionally. Forgiveness acknowledges this shared human condition and offers a way out of the cycle of hurt and retaliation, leading instead towards healing and reconciliation.

Moreover, forgiveness is a journey towards freedom. It liberates you from the heavy burdens of bitterness and grudge, freeing your mind and heart for greater peace and happiness. This liberation does not happen overnight; it is a gradual process that often requires time, patience, and persistence. Forgiveness allows you to reclaim your power, deciding that your peace and wellbeing are more important than holding onto grievances.

Importantly, forgiveness is as much about forgiving yourself as it is about forgiving others. Many of you carry guilt, shame, and self-reproach for past actions or failures. Recognizing your own need for forgiveness is a crucial step towards healing. It enables you to extend the same compassion and understanding to yourself that we are asked to offer others.

"Forgiveness as the Pathway: Healing the Mind the Body the Soul"

The true meaning of forgiveness, therefore, is not just about overcoming negative feelings towards others but about a deeper, internal transformation. It is about healing the wounds within you, reconnecting with your inherent capacity for love and compassion, and moving forward with a lighter heart and a clearer mind. Forgiveness is a pathway to inner peace and spiritual growth, a journey that enriches your life in profound and unexpected ways.

Misconceptions about forgiveness
Misconceptions about forgiveness often hinder the healing process, creating barriers that prevent people from embracing this powerful tool for personal growth and reconciliation. These misunderstandings can distort the nature of forgiveness, leading to confusion and reluctance to forgive.

Here, we address some of the common misconceptions and clarify what forgiveness truly entails.
1. Forgiveness Means Forgetting: One of the most prevalent myths is that forgiving someone requires you to forget what happened. This misconception confuses forgiveness with amnesia. In reality, forgiveness does not entail erasing memories or denying the pain caused. It is about changing how you relate to those memories, reducing their power to hurt you and learning from the experience.
2. Forgiveness Equals Condoning or Excusing Behavior: Many resist forgiveness because they believe it implies approving of or excusing the wrongful actions of others. However, acknowledging the hurtful nature of the actions and holding individuals accountable is entirely compatible with forgiveness. Forgiveness is about liberating oneself from the emotional burden of resentment, not diminishing the seriousness of the offense.
3. Forgiveness Requires Reconciliation: There is a common belief that to forgive someone, you must also reconcile and restore the relationship to its previous state. While reconciliation can be a beautiful outcome of forgiveness, it is not a requirement. Forgiveness is an internal process that can occur even if you choose to maintain distance from the person who harmed you or if reconciliation is not safe or possible.
4. Forgiveness is a Sign of Weakness: This myth portrays forgiveness as a surrender or a sign of weakness. On the contrary, forgiveness is an act of strength and courage. It takes a great deal of emotional maturity to release resentment and choose peace over holding onto hurt.

"Forgiveness as the Pathway: Healing the Mind the Body the Soul"

5. **Forgiveness Happens Instantly:** Another misconception is that forgiveness is a one-time act that happens immediately. In truth, forgiveness is a process that can take time. It involves working through complex emotions and may require revisiting the feelings of hurt as part of the healing journey.

6. **Forgiveness is Only for the Other Person:** People often think that forgiveness is something we do solely for the benefit of the person who wronged you. While forgiveness can positively affect relationships, its primary beneficiary is the forgiver. Forgiveness is a self-care practice that alleviates the emotional burden of carrying anger and bitterness.

7. **Forgiveness Means Trust is Automatically Restored:** Forgiving someone does not mean that you automatically trust them again. Trust is built over time through consistent and reliable behavior. While forgiveness can be a step towards rebuilding trust, it does not obligate one to trust the person immediately or without evidence of change.

By debunking these misconceptions, "Forgiveness as the Pathway: Healing the Mind, the Body, the Soul" aims to provide a clearer understanding of what forgiveness truly means. It empowers individuals to embrace forgiveness on their own terms, recognizing it as a powerful tool for personal liberation and healing.

The psychological and spiritual dimensions of forgiving

The act of forgiveness is a deeply transformative process that encompasses both psychological and spiritual dimensions, each playing a crucial role in the journey towards healing and inner peace. Understanding these dimensions can illuminate the profound impacts of forgiveness on our overall well-being and our connections with others and the world around us.

Psychological Dimensions of Forgiving

Psychologically, forgiveness is a complex emotional process that involves moving beyond feelings of resentment, anger, and desire for vengeance towards a state of emotional release and peace. This process can significantly impact mental health, leading to reduced stress, lower levels of anxiety and depression, and improved mood. The act of forgiving can also enhance self-esteem and lead to healthier relationships by breaking the cycle of bitterness and hostility.

The psychological process of forgiveness involves several key steps:
- **Acknowledgment of Hurt:** Recognizing and accepting the reality of the hurt experienced is the first step towards healing. This involves confronting the pain rather than denying or suppressing it.
- **Empathy Development:** Forgiveness often requires the

development of empathy towards the offender. Understanding their motives or the circumstances that led to their actions can help diminish feelings of anger and promote emotional healing.
- **Reframing the Narrative:** Individuals who forgive are able to reframe the narrative of their experience, shifting from a victim mindset to a more empowered perspective. This reframing helps in recognizing personal growth and learning that emerged from the adversity.
- **Choosing to Let Go:** Forgiveness is a choice. It involves making a conscious decision to release negative emotions and thoughts related to the offense, freeing oneself from the emotional bondage to the past.

Spiritual Dimensions of Forgiving

On a spiritual level, forgiveness is often seen as a sacred act that reflects the essence of your interconnectedness and your capacity for compassion, understanding, and unconditional love. It transcends the personal to touch upon universal themes of human existence, such as the imperfection of the human condition and the transformative power of love and compassion.

The spiritual dimensions of forgiveness include:
- **Connection to Higher Values:** Forgiveness can be an expression of higher values and virtues, such as compassion, kindness, and love. It reflects a commitment to these values, even in the face of wrongdoing.
- **Release and Renewal:** Spiritually, forgiveness is akin to a release of heavy burdens that you carry, allowing for a sense of renewal and rebirth. It opens up space within for peace, joy, and a deeper connection with the self and the divine.
- **Healing and Wholeness:** Forgiveness is often described as a pathway to healing and a return to wholeness. It helps to restore a sense of balance and harmony within oneself and in one's relationships with others and the universe.
- **Personal and Collective Transformation:** On a spiritual level, forgiveness is seen as a catalyst for personal and collective transformation. It has the power to heal not only individuals but also communities by fostering reconciliation, understanding, and peace.

These psychological and spiritual dimensions are explored to highlight how forgiveness is a multi-faceted process that nurtures your mental health, enriches your spiritual life, and fosters a sense of profound connection and harmony with the world around you. Embracing the full scope of

"Forgiveness as the Pathway: Healing the Mind the Body the Soul"

forgiveness can lead to a transformative journey that heals and liberates, offering a path to a more peaceful and fulfilling life.

As you conclude the first chapter, you are reminded of the multifaceted nature of forgiveness and its profound impact on your life. Understanding forgiveness is not merely about grasping its definition but about recognizing its power to transform hurt into healing, conflict into peace, and suffering into understanding.

Through exploring the true essence of forgiveness, addressing common misconceptions, and delving into its psychological and spiritual dimensions, we have laid the foundation for a journey that has the potential to liberate the soul from the shackles of resentment and pain. Forgiveness emerges as a courageous act of self-love and compassion, a deliberate choice that leads to freedom and inner peace.

The insights gathered in this chapter encourage you to view forgiveness not as a sign of weakness but as a profound strength. It challenges you to confront your deepest wounds and to choose a path of healing and growth. This understanding invites you to embrace forgiveness as a transformative power that can enrich your life, improve your relationships, and contribute to your overall well-being.

As you move forward, let you carry with you the lessons learned from this exploration of forgiveness. Let these insights guide you on your journey towards healing the mind, the body, and the soul. May you find the courage to forgive, the strength to let go, and the wisdom to understand that in the act of forgiving, you open your hearts to a world of peace, love, and infinite possibilities.

"Forgiveness as the Pathway: Healing the Mind, the Body, the Soul" beckons you to embark on this transformative journey with an open heart and a willing spirit, promising a path that leads not only to personal healing but to a more compassionate and understanding world.

"Forgiveness as the Pathway: Healing the Mind the Body the Soul"

Incorporating practical exercises into the exploration of forgiveness can greatly enhance the understanding and experience of its healing power. Here are three exercises designed to accompany Chapter 1 of "Forgiveness as the Pathway: Healing the Mind, the Body, the Soul," each aimed at deepening your insight into forgiveness and facilitating the beginning of your personal journey towards healing.

Exercise 1: The Forgiveness Letter
Objective: To express and process feelings of hurt and anger, and to begin the journey towards letting go.
- **Choose Someone:** Think of someone who has caused you pain or hurt, to whom you are ready to extend forgiveness.
- **Write a Letter:** Write a detailed letter to this person, expressing all the feelings of hurt, disappointment, and anger you have experienced because of their actions. Be honest and open in your expression, knowing this letter is for your eyes only.
- **Shift Towards Forgiveness:** In the latter part of the letter, start shifting your tone towards understanding and forgiveness. Reflect on any lessons learned, how you have grown, or express a desire to let go of the negative feelings.
- **Conclusion:** Conclude the letter with a statement of forgiveness or a wish for peace, either for the person or for yourself.
- **Dispose:** Ritually dispose of it (e.g., burning it safely, burying it, shredding it) as a symbolic act of letting go.

Exercise 2: The Forgiveness Meditation
Objective: To cultivate feelings of empathy and forgiveness towards someone who has wronged you.
- **Find a Quiet Space:** Sit in a quiet and comfortable place where you won't be disturbed.
- **Relaxation:** Close your eyes, take deep breaths, and allow your body to relax. Visualize each part of your body releasing tension with every exhale.
- **Visualization:** Visualize the person you want to forgive. Try to see them beyond their actions, as a fellow human being with their own struggles and pain.
- **Empathy and Understanding:** Reflect on what might have led them to act the way they did. Try to understand their actions from

a place of empathy.
- ➢ **Sending Forgiveness:** In your mind, express your forgiveness to them, saying, "I forgive you," and visualize sending them peace and understanding.
- ➢ **Releasing Pain:** Visualize yourself letting go of the pain and hurt, seeing it dissolve away with each breath.
- ➢ **Closing:** Gently bring your awareness back to the present moment, taking with you a sense of peace and release.

Exercise 3: The Self-Forgiveness Journal

Objective: To explore areas where you may need to forgive yourself, facilitating healing and self-compassion.

- ➢ **Journaling Setup:** Create a comfortable space for journaling, with a notebook and pen.
- ➢ **Prompt Reflection:** Reflect on situations where you feel you may have wronged yourself. Write about these instances, focusing on your feelings and why you think forgiveness is needed.
- ➢ **Understanding and Compassion:** For each situation, write down what you learned from the experience and how it has contributed to your growth. Offer words of understanding and compassion to yourself.
- ➢ **Affirmation of Forgiveness:** Conclude each entry with an affirmation of forgiveness towards yourself, such as, "I acknowledge my mistakes, learn from them, and forgive myself fully."
- ➢ **Reflection:** Spend a few moments in silence after journaling, reflecting on the feelings of self-compassion and forgiveness you have cultivated.

These exercises, designed to complement the insights and are stepping stones on the path to understanding and practicing forgiveness. By engaging with these exercises, you can start to experience the liberating and healing power of forgiveness in your life.

2 THE WOUNDS WITHIN

"In the quiet chambers of your heart lie the wounds you have carried, silent but profound. It is in acknowledging their existence and understanding their depth that you begin the courageous journey of healing and transformation."

As we venture deeper into "Forgiveness as the Pathway: Healing the Mind, the Body, the Soul," we turn your attention to the silent witnesses of your pain—the wounds within. These internal scars, often concealed and guarded, bear testimony to our experiences of hurt, betrayal, and disappointment. This chapter invites you to embark on a profound journey inward, to confront and understand the nature of these wounds, for it is only through recognition and acknowledgment that healing can truly begin.

The wounds within are not merely remnants of past conflicts or misunderstandings; they are intricate parts of your story that shape your perceptions, reactions, and interactions with the world. They can manifest as deep-seated feelings of inadequacy, unworthiness, or unlovability, influencing your behavior and decisions in ways you may not fully comprehend. These hidden hurts can lock you in cycles of fear, anger, and resentment, holding you back from experiencing the fullness of life.

In this chapter, we delve into the anatomy of emotional wounds, exploring their origins and the ways in which they embed themselves into the fabric of your being. We discuss the psychological impact of carrying these wounds unaddressed—how they can distort your self-image and hinder your ability to form healthy relationships. Moreover, we examine the physical toll of emotional pain, shedding light on the interconnectedness of mind and body and how unresolved emotional issues can manifest as physical ailments.

This exploration is not intended to dwell on the past or to amplify suffering but to illuminate the path toward healing. By understanding the nature of your wounds, you gain insights into your needs for love, acceptance, and forgiveness. This chapter aims to equip you with the knowledge and tools to gently probe these tender spots within, offering compassion and care to the parts of yourself that have been long neglected.

"The Wounds Within" serves as a call to bravery—a summons to face your shadows with the light of awareness and understanding. It is a step towards releasing the hold that past hurts have on you, allowing you to move forward with greater freedom and authenticity. As you learn to acknowledge and heal your internal wounds, you pave the way for a deeper, more meaningful journey of forgiveness, not just towards others, but crucially, towards yourself.

Recognizing emotional, mental, and physical wounds
Recognizing emotional, mental, and physical wounds is a critical step in the healing journey. These wounds, often interconnected, can impact every aspect of your life, shaping your interactions, your self-perception, and your overall well-being. In "Forgiveness as the Pathway: Healing the Mind, the Body, the Soul," we delve into the nuances of these wounds, understanding their origins, manifestations, and the pathways to their recognition and healing.

Emotional Wounds
Emotional wounds are injuries to your inner self, often resulting from experiences of rejection, betrayal, abandonment, neglect, or loss. These wounds can leave deep scars, affecting our ability to trust, love, and connect with others. Recognizing emotional wounds involves acknowledging the feelings of sadness, anger, fear, or shame that linger long after the triggering event has passed. Signs of emotional wounds may include persistent feelings of unworthiness, a pervasive sense of insecurity, or a deep-seated fear of abandonment.

To recognize these wounds, it is important to tune into your emotions, understanding that your reactions and sensitivities often stem from these unhealed injuries. Journaling, reflective practices, and therapy can serve as valuable tools in identifying and articulating these emotional wounds.

Mental Wounds
Mental wounds encompass the psychological impacts of traumatic experiences, including patterns of negative thinking, anxiety, depression, and PTSD. These wounds can distort your perception of reality, leading to a skewed self-image and worldview. Recognizing mental wounds requires a mindful examination of your thought patterns and behaviors, identifying those that are self-destructive or rooted in past trauma.
Symptoms of mental wounds might include recurring negative thoughts, an inability to concentrate, persistent sadness or hopelessness, and sudden

mood swings. Addressing mental wounds often necessitates professional support, such as therapy or counseling, providing a safe space to unpack these complex psychological injuries.

Physical Wounds
Physical wounds refer not only to injuries inflicted on the body but also to the somatic manifestations of emotional and mental pain. Stress, anxiety, and unresolved emotional issues can manifest as physical symptoms, including chronic pain, fatigue, gastrointestinal problems, and sleep disturbances. These physical signs are the body's way of signaling that something is amiss on a deeper level.

Recognizing physical wounds tied to emotional or mental distress involves a holistic approach to health, acknowledging the profound connection between mind and body. Practices such as yoga, meditation, and body-awareness exercises can help you tune into your body, identifying and addressing areas of pain or tension that may be linked to deeper emotional or mental wounds.

Recognizing these wounds is the first step towards healing. By bringing awareness to the presence and impact of emotional, mental, and physical wounds, you can begin to understand the full extent of their influence on your lives and embark on a deliberate path to healing and forgiveness. This process not only involves addressing the wounds themselves but also understanding the interconnectedness of your emotional, mental, and physical health as you seek wholeness and peace.

How unforgiveness affects the mind, body, and soul
Unforgiveness, the state of holding onto anger, resentment, and bitterness towards someone who has wronged you, can have profound and pervasive effects on the mind, body, and soul. This section explores the negative impact of unforgiveness, illustrating why it is essential to embark on the journey of forgiveness for holistic healing and well-being.
- *Effects on the Mind:* Unforgiveness can significantly impact mental health, leading to increased stress, anxiety, and depression. The constant rumination over past hurts keeps the mind in a state of heightened alertness and negativity, which can drain mental energy and lead to emotional exhaustion. This state of ongoing stress can impair cognitive functions, such as memory and decision-making, and can negatively affect one's outlook on life,

leading to a pessimistic and cynical worldview. The burden of unforgiveness can also hinder one's ability to form healthy, trusting relationships, as the fear of being hurt again may lead to withdrawal or defensive behavior.

- *Effects on the Body*: The psychological stress associated with unforgiveness can manifest physically in various ways. Chronic stress triggers the body's fight-or-flight response, releasing stress hormones like cortisol and adrenaline. Over time, elevated levels of these hormones can lead to a host of health issues, including high blood pressure, heart disease, a weakened immune system, and increased risk of chronic conditions such as obesity and type 2 diabetes. Moreover, the tension and stress can contribute to chronic pain, headaches, and gastrointestinal problems, as well as disturbances in sleep patterns, all of which can significantly diminish your quality of life.
- *Effects on the Soul:* At a deeper level, unforgiveness can erode the soul, affecting your sense of peace, joy, and connection to the world and others. It can lead to a feeling of being stuck or trapped, unable to move forward in life. The spiritual turmoil brought about by holding onto resentment can cloud your sense of purpose and disconnect you from your values and beliefs. This disconnection can result in a feeling of emptiness or spiritual malaise, where life seems devoid of meaning or fulfillment. Moreover, the isolation that often accompanies unforgiveness can exacerbate these feelings, leading to a profound sense of loneliness and despair.

The Cycle of Unforgiveness
Unforgiveness perpetuates a cycle of pain and suffering, where the initial wound is compounded by the ongoing harm caused by the refusal to forgive. This cycle can only be broken by the decision to embark on the path of forgiveness, a decision that, while challenging, promises a journey towards healing, freedom, and a renewed sense of connection to oneself and others.
In understanding how unforgiveness affects the mind, body, and soul, "Forgiveness as the Pathway: Healing the Mind, the Body, the Soul" underscores the importance of forgiveness as a liberating force. Forgiveness offers a way out of the cycle of pain, a pathway to healing that restores peace, promotes physical health, and rekindles the light within the soul, guiding you towards a fuller, more vibrant life.

"Forgiveness as the Pathway: Healing the Mind the Body the Soul"

The science of stress, negativity, and their impacts on health
The science behind stress, negativity, and their impacts on health is both extensive and revealing. It shows how your physical and psychological well-being is deeply interconnected with your emotional state and thought patterns. Understanding this relationship can help you appreciate the importance of managing stress and cultivating a positive outlook for your overall health.

The Physiology of Stress
When you experience stress, your body responds by activating the sympathetic nervous system, triggering the "fight-or-flight" response. This response releases stress hormones, including cortisol and adrenaline, preparing your body to face a perceived threat. While this mechanism is vital for survival, its chronic activation in response to everyday stressors can lead to detrimental health effects. Prolonged exposure to cortisol and other stress hormones can increase your risk for heart disease, hypertension, diabetes, and mental health disorders such as anxiety and depression.

Negativity and Its Physical Effects
Negative emotions and thought patterns, such as chronic anger, worry, or pessimism, can exacerbate the body's stress response. Studies have shown that individuals with a negative outlook tend to have worse health outcomes than their more optimistic counterparts. For example, negativity can weaken the immune system, making you more susceptible to infections and slowing down recovery times. Additionally, it can lead to increased inflammation in the body, a risk factor for numerous chronic conditions.

Mental Health Impacts
The impact of stress and negativity extends to mental health, influencing your risk of developing conditions like depression and anxiety. Chronic stress can alter brain function and structure, particularly in areas responsible for memory, emotion regulation, and decision-making. This can lead to difficulty concentrating, mood swings, and impaired judgment. Negativity can also reinforce these mental health issues by fostering a cycle of negative thinking that is hard to break, further impacting your quality of life.

"Forgiveness as the Pathway: Healing the Mind the Body the Soul"

Behavioral Consequences
Stress and negativity often lead to unhealthy coping mechanisms, such as overeating, physical inactivity, smoking, or substance abuse. These behaviors can compound the negative effects on health, creating a vicious cycle that is difficult to escape.

Breaking the Cycle
The good news is that interventions such as mindfulness meditation, regular physical activity, social support, and cognitive-behavioral strategies can significantly mitigate the effects of stress and negativity. These practices not only help reduce the levels of stress hormones in your body but also promote a more positive outlook on life, enhancing both mental and physical health. Cultivating a practice of appreciation, focusing on positive interactions, and seeking joy in the small things can further buffer the impacts of stress and negativity.

Understanding the science of stress, negativity, and their impacts on health highlights the importance of adopting strategies to manage stress and cultivate a positive mindset. By actively working to reduce stress and embrace a more optimistic outlook, you can significantly improve your overall well-being and quality of life.

"Forgiveness as the Pathway: Healing the Mind the Body the Soul"

Chapter 2: The Wounds Within Exercises

These exercises are designed to help you identify, understand, and begin the healing process for your emotional, mental, and physical wounds. Engaging in these activities can provide a foundation for deeper exploration and healing throughout your journey.

Exercise 1: Mapping Your Wounds

Objective: To create a visual representation of your wounds, helping to identify where they stem from and how they impact you today.

- **Materials Needed:** You will need a large sheet of paper and some colored pens or markers.
- **Draw a Tree:** On the paper, draw a large tree, including roots, a trunk, and branches. The roots represent your past experiences, the trunk symbolizes your present self, and the branches reflect your future possibilities and relationships.
- **Identify and Mark Your Wounds:** Using different colors, mark areas on the tree that represent wounds from your past (on the roots), how they affect you in the present (on the trunk), and how they might influence your future (on the branches). For each wound, write a brief note about the event or situation that caused it.
- **Reflection:** Reflect on the patterns you see. How do past wounds impact your present self and future possibilities? This exercise can help you understand the connections between your experiences and current challenges.

Exercise 2: The Healing Letter

Objective: To facilitate emotional release and begin the process of healing wounds through writing.

- **Choose a Wound:** Think of a specific wound that is particularly painful or challenging for you right now.
- **Write a Letter:** Write a letter addressed to yourself, or the person/thing that caused this wound, expressing all your feelings about the event and its impact on your life. Be honest and allow yourself to fully express the pain, anger, sadness, or any other emotions you feel.
- **Offer Compassion and Understanding:** Shift the tone of the letter towards compassion and understanding. If writing to

yourself, offer kindness and forgiveness for any mistakes or shortcomings. If writing to another, try to understand their actions and express any feelings of forgiveness or release you are ready to offer.
- **Dispose:** Ritually dispose of it (e.g., burning it safely, burying it, shredding it) as a symbolic act of letting go.

Exercise 3: Body Scan for Emotional Awareness
Objective: To connect with your body and identify any physical manifestations of your emotional wounds.
- **Find a Quiet Space:** Sit or lie down in a comfortable, quiet space where you will not be disturbed.
- **Body Scan:** Close your eyes and slowly direct your attention through each part of your body, starting from your toes and moving upwards to your head. Notice any areas of tension, discomfort, or other sensations.
- **Identify Emotions:** When you encounter a sensation, pause and explore it. Ask yourself what emotions might be connected to this physical sensation. Is there a specific wound or event linked to this feeling?
- **Breathe Into the Sensation:** Focus on breathing into any areas of discomfort, imagining each breath as a wave of healing light or energy. With each exhale, envision releasing the pain or tension held in that part of your body.

Journal: After completing the scan, take some time to journal about your experience. Note any discoveries you made about the connection between your physical sensations and emotional wounds.

3 THE JOURNEY TO FORGIVENESS

"Forgiveness is not a destination reached but a path walked, where each step forward lightens the heart and frees the soul from the shadows of the past."

Embarking on the journey to forgiveness is akin to setting out on a transformative expedition, one that leads through the rugged terrains of hurt and resentment towards the serene valleys of peace and liberation. This journey, while challenging, is essential for those seeking to heal the wounds within and to reclaim their inner harmony. It is a passage that requires courage, reflection, and an unwavering commitment to personal growth. As you step onto this path, you begin to navigate the complexities of forgiving others and, equally important, forgiving yourself.

The journey to forgiveness is not linear; it meanders through layers of emotions and memories, offering lessons of empathy, compassion, and understanding along the way. It challenges you to confront the pain that has anchored your spirit, to look beyond the actions that caused your suffering, and to see the humanity in those who have wronged you. This process of seeing, understanding, and eventually releasing the grip of past hurts is both liberating and life-affirming.

At the heart of this journey lies the powerful realization that forgiveness is a choice—a deliberate decision to free yourself from the emotional shackles of the past. This choice is not made for the sake of those who inflicted the pain but as a profound act of self-care and healing. Forgiveness does not erase the past or deny the reality of the hurt, but it offers a path forward, a way to restore peace and balance to your mind, body, and soul.

As you embark on this journey, you will discover that forgiveness is not merely about absolving others but about reclaiming your power and agency. It is about choosing not to let the actions of others define your emotional landscape or dictate your future happiness. This path will lead you through moments of deep reflection, moments where you must extend grace not only to others but also to yourself, recognizing your own imperfections and the ways in which you may have contributed to cycles of hurt.

"Forgiveness as the Pathway: Healing the Mind the Body the Soul"

This chapter invites you to explore the contours of forgiveness, to understand its challenges and rewards, and to recognize the steps you can take towards healing. It is a guide for navigating the complex emotions and situations that accompany the act of forgiving, offering practical advice and insights to support you on this journey. As you move forward, remember that the journey to forgiveness is not just about overcoming obstacles but about opening your heart to a more compassionate, peaceful, and fulfilling life.

The journey to forgiveness is a profound journey of the soul, a journey that can transform the very essence of your being. It invites you to let go of the past, to embrace the present, and to step into a future filled with greater love, understanding, and inner peace.

Empathy and understanding: Seeing from the other side
Empathy and understanding are pivotal elements in the journey to forgiveness, serving as bridges that connect the realms of hurt to healing. These qualities allow you to see beyond the surface of your pain and the actions of those who have caused it, fostering a deeper sense of compassion and connection.

Empathy: The Heart's Insight
Empathy is the ability to step into someone else's shoes, to feel what they feel and see the world from their perspective. It is an emotional resonance that acknowledges the complexity of human emotions and experiences. In the context of forgiveness, empathy involves recognizing the humanity in the person who has wronged you, understanding that they, too, are a product of their circumstances, emotions, and life experiences. This does not excuse harmful actions but offers a broader context within which those actions occurred.

Cultivating empathy starts with curiosity about the other person's experiences and motivations. It is about asking, "What pain or circumstances might have led them to act this way?" This inquiry does not diminish your own pain but acknowledges that pain and suffering are universal experiences that can lead to regrettable actions.

Here's a list of such factors that might lead someone to act in ways that hurt others:
- **Generational Patterns and Cycles:** Often, behaviors and reactions are part of generational cycles where actions and attitudes are learned and repeated. If someone has experienced hurt, neglect, or specific negative behaviors from their parents or caregivers, they

may unconsciously replicate these patterns in their own lives. This generational transmission of behavior can stem from deeply ingrained beliefs, values, and survival strategies passed down through families. Understanding this can help in recognizing that some harmful actions might not originate from a place of malice but from a cycle of behavior that the individual has been born into and may not even be fully aware of. Breaking these cycles requires awareness, intention, and often support, but recognizing their existence is a critical step in cultivating empathy and understanding for both the individual and those affected by their actions.

- **Past Trauma:** Individuals who have experienced trauma in their lives may react to current situations in ways that are influenced by past pain, leading to defensive or aggressive behaviors as coping mechanisms.
- **Stress and Pressure:** High levels of stress, whether from work, personal life, or financial issues, can lead to emotional outbursts or poor decision-making, affecting relationships negatively.
- **Mental Health Challenges:** Conditions such as depression, anxiety, or personality disorders can significantly impact a person's behavior and interactions with others.
- **Cultural and Familial Influences:** Cultural background and family dynamics play a crucial role in shaping one's behaviors and attitudes. What might be perceived as hurtful or inappropriate in one culture or family may not be seen the same way in another.
- **Lack of Emotional Intelligence:** Individuals who haven't developed the skills to identify, understand, and manage their emotions effectively might act out in hurtful ways, not fully comprehending the impact of their actions on others.
- **Misunderstandings and Miscommunication:** Many conflicts arise from misunderstandings or poor communication, where intentions are misinterpreted or messages are not clearly conveyed.
- **Insecurity and Low Self-Esteem:** Feelings of inadequacy or low self-worth can lead individuals to engage in negative behaviors towards others as a way to protect themselves or assert their worth.
- **Influence of Peers and Social Circles:** The desire to fit in or gain approval from peers can drive individuals to act against their better judgment, sometimes hurting others in the process.
- **Substance Abuse:** The use of alcohol or drugs can significantly alter a person's behavior, leading to actions they might not take when sober.
- **Ignorance or Lack of Awareness:** Sometimes, individuals may not fully understand the consequences of their actions or how they

"Forgiveness as the Pathway: Healing the Mind the Body the Soul"

affect others, acting out of ignorance rather than malice. Recognizing these and other life circumstances does not excuse harmful behavior but provides a context for understanding the complexities behind actions that cause pain. This broader perspective is crucial in the journey to forgiveness, allowing for a deeper empathy and a more comprehensive approach to healing and reconciliation.

Understanding: The Mind's Bridge
While empathy connects emotionally, understanding builds a cognitive bridge that helps rationalize why things happened the way they did. It is an intellectual process of piecing together the factors that influenced a person's behavior, which might include their upbringing, cultural background, personal struggles, or even misunderstandings. Understanding seeks to find the reasons behind actions, providing a clearer picture that can challenge the initial narrative of hurt and betrayal.

This process of seeking understanding is not about finding excuses but about searching for clarity. It is recognizing that human actions are often complicated, influenced by a web of factors that go beyond what is immediately visible. This clarity can diffuse the intensity of our negative emotions, making space for a more nuanced view of the situation.

Seeing from the Other Side
Empathy and understanding work together to enable us to see from the other side—to perceive the situation as the other person might have. This perspective shift is crucial in the forgiveness process. It allows us to move from a place of personal hurt to a broader perspective that considers the collective human experience of suffering, mistake-making, and the longing for redemption.

Seeing from the other side also means recognizing that forgiveness is a gift to oneself. It is an understanding that, while you cannot change the past, you can influence how it affects your present and future. By embracing empathy and understanding, you choose to release yourself from the cycle of hurt and resentment, opening the door to healing and peace.

The Role of Empathy and Understanding in Healing
Empathy and understanding do not negate the pain or justify the harm caused. Instead, they provide a pathway through which forgiveness can be genuinely achieved. They allow for a healing process that acknowledges the complexity of human relationships and the possibility of growth and transformation for both the forgiver and the forgiven.

In practicing empathy and seeking understanding, you not only navigate towards forgiving others but also towards a deeper self-forgiveness. This journey enriches your emotional intelligence, deepens your connections with others, and fosters a more compassionate view of the world.

The journey to forgiveness, illuminated by empathy and understanding, is a testament to the strength and resilience of the human spirit. It highlights the capacity to overcome the barriers of hurt and bitterness, paving the way for a future marked by greater understanding, connection, and inner peace.

Letting go: Steps to release the hurt and resentment
Letting go of hurt and resentment is a crucial phase in the journey to forgiveness, marking the transition from being anchored in past pain to moving forward with a lighter heart. This process involves several steps, each designed to facilitate the release of negative emotions and the cultivation of peace and acceptance.

> - **Acknowledge Your Feelings:** The first step is to fully acknowledge your feelings of hurt, anger, and resentment. Recognizing these emotions without judgment allows you to validate your experiences and understand that your feelings are a natural response to being wronged. This acknowledgment is essential for healing to begin.
> - **Reflect on the Impact:** Consider how holding onto these negative emotions affects your life. Reflect on the impact that resentment and anger have on your mental health, physical well-being, relationships, and overall quality of life. Understanding the cost of unforgiveness can motivate you to initiate the process of letting go.
> - **Decide to Let Go:** Making a conscious decision to let go of hurt and resentment is a pivotal moment in your healing journey. This decision is not about condoning the actions of others but about choosing not to allow those actions to control your emotions and life any longer. It is a commitment to prioritizing your peace and well-being.
> - **Practice Empathy and Understanding:** As discussed earlier, cultivating empathy and understanding towards the person who has hurt you can be instrumental in the process of letting go. This involves seeing the situation from their perspective, acknowledging any external factors that may have influenced their behavior, and recognizing their humanity.
> - **Express Your Feelings:** Finding a safe and constructive way to express your feelings can be a cathartic part of the letting-go process. This might involve writing a letter (which you don't have

to send), talking to a trusted friend or therapist, or engaging in creative activities like painting or music.
- **Seek Closure:** Closure can come in many forms and does not necessarily require reconciliation with the person who wronged you. It might involve creating a ritual to say goodbye to your pain, setting boundaries for future interactions, or simply making peace with the fact that some questions may remain unanswered.
- **Focus on the Present and Future:** Shift your focus from the past to the present and future. Engage in activities that bring you joy, cultivate positive relationships, and set goals for the future. Focusing on what you can control and the positive aspects of your life can help dilute the bitterness of past hurts.
- **Practice Appreciation:** Cultivating a practice of appreciation can significantly shift your perspective from one of loss and hurt to one of appreciation and abundance. Regularly reflecting on the things you are thankful for can decrease feelings of resentment and facilitate emotional healing.
- **Self-Care and Compassion:** Taking care of yourself physically, emotionally, and spiritually is crucial during this time. Engage in activities that nurture your well-being, such as exercise, meditation, spending time in nature, or pursuing hobbies. Treat yourself with the same compassion and kindness that you would offer a friend in pain.
- **Forgive:** Ultimately, letting go culminates in forgiveness. Remember, forgiveness is a process and a choice that might need to be revisited several times. It is not a sign of weakness but a powerful act of self-liberation.

Letting go of hurt and resentment is a transformative process that frees you from the weight of the past, allowing you to embrace a future filled with possibility, peace, and happiness. While the journey may be challenging, the freedom and clarity that come from releasing these burdens are profoundly rewarding, opening the door to a more fulfilling and vibrant life.

4 FORGIVENESS AND HEALING THE MIND

"Forgiveness is the key that unlocks the door to mental freedom, transforming the chains of past hurts into wings of wisdom and peace."

Embarking on the journey of forgiveness brings us to a critical juncture where we explore its profound impact on mental health. This chapter delves into the intricate process of how forgiveness acts as a catalyst for healing the mind, unraveling the bonds of past hurts to restore peace, clarity, and wellbeing. The act of forgiving—whether it is others or oneself—is not just an emotional release but also a psychological transformation that redefines your inner narratives and liberates you from the chains of negative thought patterns.

The mind, a complex and delicate tapestry woven with memories, emotions, and thoughts, is often the battleground where the struggle to forgive unfolds. The scars of betrayal, disappointment, and hurt can embed themselves deeply within your psyche, influencing how you perceive the world and yourself. Left unaddressed, these wounds can fester, giving rise to anger, resentment, bitterness, and a host of mental health challenges, including anxiety, depression, and chronic stress. Forgiveness offers a pathway out of this tumultuous landscape, guiding you towards healing and mental freedom.

This chapter explores the transformative power of forgiveness on the mind, highlighting the psychological shifts that occur when you choose to let go of resentment. It delves into the science behind forgiveness, illustrating how this act can decrease stress, enhance emotional resilience, and lead to greater happiness and satisfaction in life. Through forgiveness, you can break the cycle of rumination and negative thinking that holds you captive to your past experiences, opening the door to new possibilities and perspectives.

Forgiveness also fosters greater self-awareness and empathy, allowing you to understand and connect with others on a deeper level. It challenges you to confront your vulnerabilities and fears, encouraging growth and self-compassion. As you learn to forgive, you also learn to embrace your imperfections, recognizing that growth often stems from your struggles and missteps.

Moreover, this chapter offers practical guidance and strategies to facilitate the process of forgiveness, providing tools to navigate the emotional complexities involved. From mindfulness and reflective practices to cognitive-behavioral techniques, you will discover a variety of approaches to support your journey towards healing the mind. These practices not only aid in the process of forgiveness but also contribute to overall mental wellness, enhancing your ability to cope with life's challenges and uncertainties.

As you journey through this chapter, it becomes evident that forgiveness is not merely an act of kindness towards others; it is an essential step towards self-healing and mental well-being. It requires courage, patience, and persistence but yields profound rewards for those willing to embark on this transformative path. By forgiving, you do not change the past, but you do change the future—freeing your mind to experience the richness of life with a renewed sense of peace and openness.

Mental health benefits of forgiving

The act of forgiving is often seen through a moral or ethical lens, but its benefits extend far into the realm of mental health. Embracing forgiveness can lead to significant psychological well-being and improvement in your overall quality of life. This process, while challenging, fosters a profound transformation within the mind, paving the way for healing, resilience, and a deeper sense of peace.

Reduction in Negative Emotions

One of the most immediate benefits of forgiveness is the reduction of negative emotions. Holding onto anger, resentment, or bitterness can be emotionally exhausting, keeping the mind in a constant state of turmoil. Forgiveness allows these negative emotions to dissipate, replaced by feelings of compassion and understanding. This emotional shift can significantly lower stress levels, reduce anxiety, and decrease the risk of depression, contributing to a more balanced and positive emotional state.

Enhanced Psychological Resilience

Forgiving builds psychological resilience, equipping you with the skills to navigate future conflicts and setbacks more effectively. It fosters a sense of personal empowerment by moving from a victim mindset to one of agency and control. This resilience is rooted in the understanding that while you cannot control the actions of others, you have the choice in how you respond and the meanings you assign to your experiences. As a result, you become more adaptable, capable of facing life's challenges with a sense of confidence and strength.

Improved Self-Esteem
Forgiveness is intricately linked to self-esteem. Harboring resentment often leads to self-critical thoughts and a focus on personal faults and vulnerabilities. In contrast, forgiving encourages a kinder self-view, recognizing that everyone makes mistakes and deserves compassion, including yourself. This gentler self-perception can significantly boost self-esteem, fostering a healthier relationship with oneself.

Better Relationships
The practice of forgiveness can also lead to improved relationships. It promotes open communication, empathy, and understanding, essential components of healthy and supportive relationships. Forgiving and seeking forgiveness when necessary creates a foundation of trust and mutual respect, allowing relationships to deepen and thrive. Moreover, the skills developed through forgiving—such as empathy, communication, and emotional regulation—benefit not only personal relationships but professional and casual interactions as well.

Increased Happiness and Life Satisfaction
At its core, forgiveness is linked to increased happiness and life satisfaction. By releasing the burden of negative emotions and embracing a more positive outlook, you often find a greater appreciation for life. This renewed perspective can open the door to joy, appreciation, and a deeper sense of fulfillment. Studies have shown that individuals who practice forgiveness report higher levels of happiness, more satisfaction with life, and lower levels of stress and psychological distress.

Improved Physical Health
While primarily benefiting mental health, forgiveness also contributes to better physical health, a testament to the mind-body connection. Stress and negative emotions associated with unforgiveness can lead to physical ailments, as previously discussed. Therefore, by fostering forgiveness, individuals can also experience improvements in physical health, including lower blood pressure, improved heart health, and a stronger immune system.

The mental health benefits of forgiving are profound and far-reaching. By

"Forgiveness as the Pathway: Healing the Mind the Body the Soul"

choosing to forgive, you embark on a journey of healing that not only alleviates the burden of negative emotions but also fosters growth, resilience, and a deeper sense of inner peace. This transformative process enriches your life, promoting a healthier, more joyful existence rooted in compassion and understanding.

"Forgiveness as the Pathway: Healing the Mind the Body the Soul"

Forgiveness as therapy: Techniques and Practices

Forgiveness can be a therapeutic journey, offering profound healing and restoration for those burdened by resentment, anger, or guilt. Viewing forgiveness through the lens of therapy opens up a myriad of techniques and practices designed to facilitate this complex process. These methods aim to address emotional wounds at their core, allowing individuals to release the hold of past hurts and move forward with greater peace and clarity.

- **Cognitive-Behavioral Techniques**

Cognitive-behavioral therapy (CBT) offers valuable strategies for fostering forgiveness, focusing on altering negative thought patterns and beliefs that fuel resentment and anger. Through CBT, you learn to challenge and reframe these thoughts, gradually shifting their perspective on the person or situation that caused them harm. Techniques such as journaling to identify and counteract negative thoughts and practicing empathy exercises to understand the other person's perspective, are commonly employed.

- **Narrative Therapy**

Narrative therapy helps you re-author your story in a way that places forgiveness and understanding at the forefront. By viewing your experiences through a new lens, you can change your relationship with past events, seeing yourself not as victims but as a survivor or even hero of your story. This shift can significantly ease the process of forgiveness, as it emphasizes growth and empowerment over hurt and victimization.

- **Mindfulness and Meditation**

Mindfulness and meditation practices are powerful tools in the journey of forgiveness. These practices foster a state of present-moment awareness and non-judgmental acceptance, creating the emotional space needed to process and release negative emotions. Loving-kindness meditation (metta) is particularly effective, as it cultivates feelings of compassion and goodwill towards oneself and others, including those who have caused hurt.

- **Expressive Therapies**

Expressive therapies, such as art therapy, music therapy, and writing, provide creative outlets for expressing and working through feelings related to unforgiveness. These modalities can help you access and process emotions that may be difficult to articulate verbally, offering a unique pathway to understanding and forgiveness. For example, writing a letter of forgiveness (whether or not it is sent) can be a cathartic exercise that allows for the expression of hurt and the articulation of a desire to forgive.

"Forgiveness as the Pathway: Healing the Mind the Body the Soul"

- **Interpersonal Therapy**

Interpersonal therapy (IPT) focuses on improving communication skills and enhancing relationships, which can be instrumental in the forgiveness process. IPT can help you express your feelings of hurt and betrayal in a healthy and constructive manner, work through conflicts, and rebuild trust. This approach is particularly beneficial when forgiveness involves direct interaction and reconciliation with the person who caused the pain.

- **Compassion-Focused Therapy**

Compassion-focused therapy (CFT) emphasizes the development of self-compassion as a foundation for extending forgiveness to others. By nurturing a compassionate and forgiving attitude towards oneself, you can more easily overcome feelings of shame, guilt, and self-criticism that may be obstacles to forgiving others. Exercises in CFT often include guided meditations focused on cultivating compassion and understanding both for oneself and others.

- **Group Therapy**

Group therapy provides a supportive environment where you can share your experiences of hurt and forgiveness with others facing similar challenges. This collective experience can offer new insights, foster empathy, and provide a sense of community and support that is invaluable in the forgiveness process.

Each of these therapeutic techniques and practices offers a unique approach to navigating the complexities of forgiveness. Whether undertaken independently or with the guidance of a therapist, they can provide the tools and support needed to heal emotional wounds, release resentment, and embrace a more forgiving and peaceful state of mind.

"Forgiveness as the Pathway: Healing the Mind the Body the Soul"

Stories of mental transformation through forgiveness

Stories of mental transformation through forgiveness underscore the profound impact that letting go of resentment and embracing forgiveness can have on one's mental and emotional well-being. These narratives highlight the journey from pain and anger to peace and understanding, illustrating the transformative power of forgiveness in healing the mind and spirit.

- **From Resentment to Peace:** One compelling story is of a person who harbored deep resentment towards a close friend who betrayed their trust. This resentment consumed their thoughts, leading to anxiety and depression. The turning point came when they decided to engage in mindfulness and compassion exercises, focusing on understanding the circumstances that led to their friend's actions. Over time, they found the strength to forgive, which led to a significant reduction in their anxiety and depression symptoms. This act of forgiveness did not excuse the behavior but allowed them to release the emotional burden they had been carrying, leading to a profound sense of peace and mental clarity.

- **Breaking the Cycle of Anger:** Another story involves an individual who grew up in a household where anger and criticism were the norm. This environment led them to develop similar patterns of behavior, affecting their relationships and personal well-being. Recognizing the need for change, they sought therapy, where they learned about the concept of generational patterns and the power of forgiveness. By forgiving their parents and understanding the origins of their behavior, they were able to break the cycle of anger, leading to improved relationships and a healthier, more positive outlook on life.

- **Healing from Past Trauma:** A remarkable transformation story is of a person who experienced significant trauma in their childhood, which left deep emotional scars. The trauma affected their self-esteem, relationships, and ability to trust others. Through a combination of narrative therapy and expressive writing, they began the process of forgiving those responsible for their pain. This journey was challenging but ultimately liberating, as it allowed them to rewrite their story from a victim to a survivor. This mental shift led to a significant improvement in their mental health, fostering a sense of empowerment and resilience that had been absent for years.

- **Reconciliation and Restoration:** A powerful example of forgiveness's impact involves two siblings estranged for years due to a misunderstanding and subsequent conflict. The rift led to feelings of loneliness, regret, and sadness in both their lives. Encouraged by a mutual friend, they began a dialogue, each taking steps to understand the other's perspective and express their own feelings of hurt. This process of communication and forgiveness led to a reconciliation that healed not just their relationship but their individual mental health, reducing feelings o' isolation and increasing their overall happiness.

These stories of mental transformation through forgiveness illuminate the profound changes that can occur when individuals choose to forgive. They underscore forgiveness's role not just in mending relationships but in promoting mental health, offering insights into how releasing resentment and embracing understanding can lead to a more fulfilling and peaceful life. Each story is a testament to the strength and resilience of the human spirit, highlighting forgiveness as a powerful tool for healing and transformation.

As we conclude Chapter 4, it is evident that the journey of forgiveness is not just an emotional or moral endeavor but a profound therapeutic process that can heal the mind in remarkable ways. The stories of transformation and the exploration of various therapeutic techniques underscore forgiveness's pivotal role in overcoming resentment, breaking free from the past, and fostering mental wellness.

Forgiveness, as you have seen, offers a path to release the heavy burdens of anger, hurt, and betrayal that weigh on your mind, contributing to stress, anxiety, and depression. By choosing to forgive, you allow yourself to move beyond the pain, opening your heart to healing and your mind to peace. This choice is a powerful act of self-care, one that restores your mental balance and enriches your emotional landscape.

The techniques and practices highlighted in this chapter—from cognitive-behavioral strategies and narrative therapy to mindfulness, compassion-focused therapy, and more—provide practical tools for navigating the complex journey of forgiveness. These approaches not only facilitate the process of letting go but also enhance your overall psychological resilience, enabling you to face future challenges with greater strength and equanimity.

Moreover, the stories shared in this chapter illustrate the transformative power of forgiveness in real-life contexts. They remind you that, while the journey may be challenging and fraught with emotional hurdles, the outcome is invariably one of profound personal growth and liberation.

"Forgiveness as the Pathway: Healing the Mind the Body the Soul"

These narratives serve as beacons of hope, demonstrating that forgiveness can lead to renewed happiness, improved relationships, and a deeper sense of life satisfaction.

In embracing forgiveness, you do not forget the past, nor do you condone wrongdoing. Instead, you choose to heal from your wounds and free yourself from the chains of negative emotions that bind you. This act of forgiveness is an investment in your mental health, a commitment to nurturing your mind, and a step toward a more joyful and peaceful existence.

As you move forward from Chapter 4, carry with you the understanding that forgiveness is a key to mental healing, a gateway to inner peace, and a cornerstone of emotional well-being. By cultivating forgiveness, you open yourself to the possibility of transformation, not just within your mind but in every aspect of your life, paving the way for a future filled with greater understanding, compassion, and love.

"Forgiveness as the Pathway: Healing the Mind the Body the Soul"

5 FORGIVENESS AND HEALING THE BODY

"Forgiveness is the soul's medicine, offering healing to the body as it releases the heart's burdens, allowing every breath to nourish us with the light of peace and renewal."

In the journey of healing, the profound interconnectedness between the mind and body plays a pivotal role. Just as your thoughts and emotions can influence your physical health, the act of forgiveness can usher in a powerful healing process within the body. This chapter delves into the remarkable ways in which forgiveness extends beyond the realms of emotional and mental liberation to foster physical healing and well-being. It explores the notion that harboring unforgiveness is not just a burden to the psyche but also to the body, manifesting in various physical ailments and stress-related conditions.

The science of psychoneuroimmunology has illuminated the pathways through which emotional and psychological stressors can impact physical health. Negative emotions like anger, resentment, and bitterness can trigger the body's stress response, leading to a cascade of physiological effects detrimental to health. Forgiveness acts as a salve, not only soothing the emotional wounds but also alleviating the physical manifestations of stress and negativity.

This chapter examines the tangible benefits of forgiveness on the body, including reduced risk of chronic diseases, lower blood pressure, improved heart health, and a stronger immune system. It highlights research findings that underscore the healing potential of forgiveness, showcasing how letting go of negative emotions can lead to a reduction in pain, improvements in sleep quality, and an overall enhancement of physical health.

Moreover, we explore practical strategies and techniques that can facilitate the process of forgiveness, thereby promoting bodily healing. These include mindfulness practices, physical activity, expressive writing, and guided imagery—all tools that can help bridge the gap between emotional forgiveness and physical health.

Personal stories of transformation further illuminate the profound impact forgiveness can have on the body. These narratives offer inspiration and insight, showing how individuals have overcome physical symptoms and improved their health outcomes through the power of forgiveness. From chronic pain dissolving as emotional burdens are lifted to improved cardiovascular health following the release of deep-seated anger, these

"Forgiveness as the Pathway: Healing the Mind the Body the Soul"

stories attest to the healing power of forgiveness.

As you navigate through this chapter, you come to understand that forgiveness is not merely an act of emotional generosity but a key component of holistic health. It invites you to consider health not just in physical terms but as an integrated state of well-being that encompasses mind, body, and spirit. Forgiveness, therefore, emerges as a critical element in the pursuit of a healthy, balanced, and vibrant life.

By embracing forgiveness, you embark on a path that leads not only to emotional and mental liberation but also to physical healing and renewal. This chapter invites you to explore the transformative impact of forgiveness on the body, offering guidance, strategies, and inspiration for those seeking to heal wholly and completely.

The body's response to letting go
The act of letting go and embracing forgiveness can have a profound and beneficial impact on the body, illustrating the intricate connection between your emotional state and physical health. This process of release initiates a series of physiological changes and improvements in bodily functions, highlighting the body's remarkable capacity for healing and renewal when freed from the burden of negative emotions.

- **Reduction in Stress Hormones:** Holding on activates the body's stress response, leading to the release of stress hormones like cortisol and adrenaline. These hormones, while useful in short-term fight-or-flight situations, can be harmful when persistently elevated, contributing to a range of health issues. Letting go helps to mitigate this stress response, leading to a reduction in the levels of these hormones. The result is a decrease in the risk of stress-related conditions such as hypertension, heart disease, and metabolic disorders.
- **Lower Blood Pressure:** The act of forgiveness and the subsequent reduction in negative emotions can lead to lower blood pressure. High blood pressure is a significant risk factor for cardiovascular disease and stroke, so this effect of forgiveness provides a direct benefit to heart health. The relaxation and easing of emotional tension that come with forgiveness help regulate blood pressure to healthier levels.

- ➤ **Improved Immune Function:** Chronic stress and negative emotions can suppress the immune system, making the body more susceptible to infections and disease. By letting go, individuals can experience an improvement in immune function. This enhanced immunity is reflected in better overall health, fewer illnesses, and a more robust response to pathogens.
- ➤ **Decrease in Chronic Pain:** For those suffering from chronic pain, forgiveness may offer a pathway to relief. Emotional distress and anger can exacerbate pain perception, while forgiveness can lead to its alleviation. The psychological relief that comes from releasing can translate into physical relief, reducing the intensity of pain and improving the quality of life for those with chronic pain conditions.
- ➤ **Enhanced Sleep Quality:** The stress and turmoil caused by holding on can interfere with sleep, leading to insomnia and poor sleep quality. Forgiveness, on the other hand, can promote relaxation and peace of mind, making it easier to fall asleep and stay asleep. Improved sleep not only enhances physical health but also supports emotional and mental well-being.
- ➤ **Promoting Longevity:** By reducing the risk factors associated with chronic stress and negative emotional states, forgiveness may indirectly contribute to a longer, healthier life. The cumulative effect of lowered blood pressure, improved immune function, reduced risk of heart disease, and better sleep can add years to your life, offering not just quantity but quality of life.

The body's response to letting go underscores the power of forgiveness as a healing force. This transformative act not only liberates the mind and soul but also brings about tangible improvements in physical health. Through forgiveness, you can unlock a pathway to a more balanced, healthy, and fulfilling life, demonstrating the remarkable capacity of the body to heal in conjunction with the mind and spirit.

"Forgiveness as the Pathway: Healing the Mind the Body the Soul"

Integrating physical health with emotional well-being

Integrating physical health with emotional well-being is a holistic approach to healing and wellness that recognizes the inseparable connection between the body and the mind. This approach suggests that to achieve optimal health, you must address both physical symptoms and emotional states. The journey of forgiveness plays a crucial role in this integration, serving as a bridge that connects emotional liberation with physical health improvements.

Understanding the Mind-Body Connection

The foundation of integrating physical health with emotional well-being lies in understanding the mind-body connection. This concept, supported by decades of research, posits that your thoughts, feelings, attitudes, and beliefs can positively or negatively affect our biological functioning. In reverse, the condition of your body can influence your mental state. Stress, anxiety, and harbored resentment can manifest as physical symptoms, while physical ailments can lead to emotional distress. Recognizing this interplay is the first step toward healing both aspects simultaneously.

The Role of Forgiveness in Integration

Forgiveness facilitates this integration by directly addressing the emotional roots of physical symptoms. By forgiving and healing emotional wounds, you can significantly reduce stress and negative emotions, leading to improved physical health outcomes. Forgiveness lowers the body's stress response, decreases inflammation, and enhances immune function, directly benefiting physical health. At the same time, the emotional relief and peace of mind that come with forgiveness contribute to a more positive mental state, further promoting overall well-being.

Practices for Integration

Several practices can help you integrate your physical health with emotional well-being:

- **Mindfulness and Meditation:** Engaging in mindfulness meditation can reduce stress and promote emotional healing, with direct benefits to physical health, such as lowered blood pressure and improved immune response.
- **Yoga and Tai Chi:** These practices combine physical movement with breath control and meditation, offering a holistic approach to stress reduction and emotional regulation, while also enhancing physical fitness and flexibility.
- **Expressive Writing:** Journaling about feelings of forgiveness or unresolved conflicts can provide emotional release and clarity, reducing stress and potentially mitigating its physical

"Forgiveness as the Pathway: Healing the Mind the Body the Soul"

manifestations.
- **Physical Activity:** Regular exercise not only improves physical health but also boosts mood and reduces symptoms of anxiety and depression, demonstrating the close link between physical activity and emotional well-being.
- **Nutrition:** A balanced diet supports both physical health and mood regulation. Certain nutrients, such as omega-3 fatty acids, vitamins, and minerals, have been linked to lower levels of depression and anxiety.
- **Social Support and Connection:** Maintaining healthy relationships and seeking support from friends, family, or support groups can improve both emotional and physical health, emphasizing the social aspect of holistic well-being.

The Impact of Integration

Integrating physical health with emotional well-being through forgiveness and supportive practices can have a transformative impact on your life. It can lead to a more balanced state of health, where emotional healing is reflected in physical vitality, and physical well-being supports mental and emotional stability. This holistic approach not only addresses specific ailments or emotional challenges but also promotes a comprehensive state of health that encompasses the entire being.

In summary, integrating physical health with emotional well-being is a multifaceted approach to wellness that acknowledges the complex interplay between the body and the mind. Through forgiveness and a variety of supportive practices, you can embark on a journey of comprehensive healing that leads to a more fulfilled, healthy, and balanced life.

Practices for embodying forgiveness

Embodying forgiveness is a holistic practice that involves integrating the act of forgiveness into your daily lives impacting your emotional, mental, and physical states. This approach to forgiveness is about more than just an intellectual decision or emotional release; it is about living in a way that reflects a genuine letting go of resentment and embracing compassion and understanding. Here are several practices that can help embody forgiveness:

> **Mindfulness Meditation:** Mindfulness meditation is a powerful tool for cultivating awareness and presence, which are essential for recognizing and releasing grudges. Through mindfulness, you can observe your thoughts and feelings without judgment, learning to let go of anger and resentment gradually. Loving-kindness meditation, a specific form of mindfulness practice, encourages you to send feelings of love and kindness to yourself, those you have

forgiven, and even those you find challenging to forgive.
- **Expressive Writing:** Writing can be a therapeutic activity that helps you articulate the emotions and thoughts surrounding the need for forgiveness. By journaling about your experiences and feelings, you can gain insights into the nature of your grievances and the steps you might take toward forgiveness. Writing letters of forgiveness, whether they are sent or not, can also be a powerful exercise in clarifying and expressing your forgiveness.
- **Physical Release Exercises:** Physical activity can be a conduit for releasing the emotional and physical tension that accompanies unforgiveness. Activities like yoga, tai chi, walking in nature, or even vigorous exercise can help release the body's stress and foster a sense of well-being. These activities not only improve physical health but can also create mental clarity and emotional relief, making it easier to process and embody forgiveness.
- **Appreciation Practices:** Cultivating appreciation shifts the focus from what has hurt you to the blessings in your life, facilitating a more forgiving outlook. Keeping an appreciation journal, where you regularly record things you are thankful for, can significantly improve your mood and outlook, making it easier to forgive. Practicing appreciation can transform your perspective, encouraging a more compassionate and forgiving stance toward yourself and others.
- **Social Support and Community Engagement:** Surrounding yourself with a supportive community or engaging in group activities can foster a sense of belonging and understanding. Participating in support groups, community service, or group therapy can provide a space to share experiences and learn from others' journeys of forgiveness. This social support is invaluable for reinforcing the practice of forgiveness in your life.
- **Rituals and Symbolic Acts:** Creating personal rituals or engaging in symbolic acts can mark significant moments in your forgiveness journey, offering closure and a physical manifestation of your internal process. This could be as simple as lighting a candle in honor of your decision to forgive, releasing a written note into a river, or planting a tree as a symbol of growth and renewal. Such acts can serve as powerful reminders of your commitment to living a life characterized by forgiveness.

"Forgiveness as the Pathway: Healing the Mind the Body the Soul"

> ➤ **Self-Compassion Exercises:** Practicing self-compassion is crucial in the process of forgiveness, especially when forgiving yourself. Techniques such as speaking to yourself with kindness, acknowledging your common humanity, and being mindful of your critical inner voice can help foster self-forgiveness. Exercises like writing a compassionate letter to yourself can be particularly healing.

By integrating these practices into your daily life, you begin to embody forgiveness, transforming it from a concept into a lived experience. This approach not only facilitates deeper emotional healing but also promotes physical health and well-being, demonstrating the profound impact of forgiveness on your overall quality of life. Through consistent practice, embodying forgiveness becomes a pathway to a more peaceful, healthy, and harmonious existence.

6 FORGIVENESS AND HEALING THE SOUL
"In the quiet sanctuary of the soul, forgiveness is the light that dissolves all shadows, illuminating a path to profound peace and spiritual renewal."

At the heart of every act of forgiveness lies a profound journey of the soul, a voyage that transcends mere emotional release to touch the very essence of your being. This chapter delves into the sacred process of forgiveness and its unparalleled power to heal the soul, inviting you on an exploration that goes beyond the surface of your wounds to the deeper spiritual scars they leave behind. In the quiet spaces of your innermost self, where pain and peace coexist, forgiveness emerges as a transformative force, capable of mending the fragmented parts of your spirit and guiding you towards wholeness and harmony.

The soul, with its innate wisdom and resilience, bears the imprints of every hurt, betrayal, and loss you endure, holding onto these memories in the shadows of your consciousness. Yet, it is also here, in the depths of your soul, that the potential for true healing and liberation resides. Forgiveness is the key that unlocks this potential, a sacred act that dissolves the chains of resentment and bitterness, allowing light to penetrate the darkness and initiate a process of profound healing.

This journey of forgiveness is both personal and universal, reflecting the shared human experience of seeking meaning, connection, and redemption in the face of suffering. It challenges you to confront your deepest fears and vulnerabilities, to release the grip of past hurts, and to open your heart to the possibilities of love and compassion. As you embark on this path, you discover that forgiving others—and yourself—is not a sign of weakness but a testament to the strength of the human spirit, a courageous choice that elevates you to higher states of understanding and grace.

In this chapter, you explore the spiritual dimensions of forgiveness, examining how this act of mercy can restore balance to your inner world, renew your sense of purpose, and deepen your connection to the divine. Through reflections on the nature of the soul and practical guidance for cultivating forgiveness in your life, you uncover the layers of healing that forgiveness can bring. You learn that to forgive is to release yourself from the burden of the past, to embrace the present with openness and appreciation, and to step into the future with hope and renewed vitality. Forgiveness and healing the soul is not a journey you undertake alone; it is

"Forgiveness as the Pathway: Healing the Mind the Body the Soul"

supported by the unseen forces of love and compassion that bind us all. It is a sacred dialogue between the human and the divine, a dance of light and shadow that reveals the beauty and resilience of the soul. As you navigate the complexities of forgiveness, you find that it is not just a path to healing but a gateway to a more profound and meaningful existence.

This chapter invites you to embark on this sacred journey of forgiveness, to explore the depths of your soul, and to discover the peace and liberation that await when you choose to forgive. It is an invitation to transform your pain into wisdom, your resentment into compassion, and your wounds into sources of strength and inspiration. In the sanctuary of the soul, forgiveness is the light that guides you home, leading you to a place of profound peace and spiritual renewal.

The spiritual journey of forgiveness
The spiritual journey of forgiveness is an odyssey that transcends the physical realm, taking you into the depths of your soul and the essence of your being. It is a path marked not by milestones of the material world but by transformations of the heart and spirit. This journey is both deeply personal and universally resonant, touching upon the core of what it means to be human—your capacity for love, compassion, and renewal in the face of pain and transgression.

At its heart, the spiritual journey of forgiveness is about connection—to oneself, to others, and to the divine or the universal energies that bind all existence. It asks you to confront your deepest wounds, not to relive the pain but to understand its origins and transcend its hold on you. This process requires a profound leap of faith, a willingness to dive into the unknown waters of your own heart with the belief that healing and redemption await on the other side.

Forgiveness, in this spiritual context, becomes an act of liberation. It frees you from the chains of resentment, anger, and bitterness that tether your souls to past hurts, preventing you from experiencing the fullness of the present moment and the boundless possibilities of the future. When you forgive, you release not just the weight of past grievances but also the limitations you have imposed on your heart and spirit. You open yourself to a higher state of consciousness, one that recognizes the impermanence of suffering and the eternal nature of love.

"Forgiveness as the Pathway: Healing the Mind the Body the Soul"

This journey often unfolds in stages, beginning with a recognition of pain and the acknowledgment of its impact on your life. It moves through the challenging waters of empathy and understanding, asking you to see your offenders through the lens of compassion, to recognize their humanity and the circumstances that led them to cause harm. This step is not about excusing their actions but about expanding your heart to encompass a broader perspective of human fallibility and the transformative power of mercy.

As you travel further along this path, you encounter the act of surrender—a pivotal moment where you let go of your need for retribution or acknowledgment of your pain. Surrender is not about defeat but about acknowledging that your healing and peace are not contingent on external validation or change. It is a profound acceptance of what is, coupled with a trust in the higher forces at work in your life.

The culmination of the spiritual journey of forgiveness is a profound renewal of the soul. It is a rebirth, marked by a deep sense of peace, a reconnection with your inner divinity, and a renewed sense of purpose. You emerge from this journey transformed, carrying within you the wisdom of your experiences and the light of forgiveness that illuminates your path forward.

Throughout this spiritual odyssey, practices such as meditation, reflection, and rituals can serve as guides and companions, helping you navigate the complexities of forgiveness. These practices ground you in the present moment, connect you with the divine, and support you in the process of letting go and moving forward.

The spiritual journey of forgiveness is a testament to the resilience of the human spirit and its capacity for growth, healing, and transcendence. It is a reminder that forgiveness is not just an act of kindness toward others but a profound gesture of self-love and respect. In forgiving, you reclaim your power, honor your journey, and open your heart to the infinite possibilities of love and connection that define your existence.

"Forgiveness as the Pathway: Healing the Mind the Body the Soul"

The Inner Work of Forgiveness

The Inner Work of Forgiveness is a profound and deeply personal journey, one that beckons you to venture into the innermost sanctums of your being, to confront and heal the wounds that reside there. This journey is about much more than overcoming resentment or extending pardon to those who have wronged you; it is a transformative pilgrimage towards self-awareness, liberation, and renewal. It demands a courageous exploration of the self, a willingness to face the shadows and illuminate them with the light of understanding and compassion.

Unveiling the Layers

The process begins with peeling back the layers of hurt, anger, and betrayal that have shrouded your heart. This unveiling is a delicate endeavor, requiring patience and gentle persistence. It is about acknowledging the pain without allowing it to define you, recognizing that beneath the layers of hurt lies a core of strength and resilience. Through practices like meditation and reflective journaling, you can begin to access these deeper layers, offering them the attention and compassion they have been denied.

Confronting the Ego

Central to the inner work of forgiveness is the confrontation with the ego—the aspect of the self that clings to grievances as a means of protection and identity. The ego resists forgiveness, fearing the vulnerability that comes with letting go. Challenging the ego involves questioning the stories you have told yourself about your hurt, seeing them not as absolute truths but as perspectives that can be shifted. This confrontation is not a battle but a negotiation, one that invites the ego to loosen its grip and consider the freedom that forgiveness offers.

Cultivating Compassion and Empathy

At the heart of forgiveness is the cultivation of compassion and empathy, both for yourself and others. This requires you to step beyond the confines of your own experience and consider the broader human condition—your shared vulnerabilities, fears, and desires. Through practices like loving-kindness meditation, you can nurture a sense of connectedness and goodwill that transcends individual grievances. Compassion becomes the bridge that connects the hurt you have experienced with the understanding that everyone, in some way, faces their own struggles.

"Forgiveness as the Pathway: Healing the Mind the Body the Soul"

The Role of Self-Forgiveness
Integral to the inner work of forgiveness is the act of forgiving oneself. This can often be the most challenging aspect, as it demands facing your own mistakes, failures, and shortcomings with honesty and kindness. Self-forgiveness is about acknowledging your humanity, accepting that imperfection is part of the human experience. It involves a deliberate release of self-judgment and the cultivation of self-compassion, recognizing that growth and learning are born from our missteps and flaws.

Embracing Transformation
The culmination of the inner work of forgiveness is a profound personal transformation—a shift in how you relate to yourself, others, and the world. This transformation is marked by a sense of liberation, a release from the chains of past hurts that have weighed down your spirit. It opens up new pathways for growth, connection, and peace, illuminating a future where forgiveness is not just an occasional act but a way of being.

Through this journey, you discover that forgiveness is a powerful act of self-love and a pivotal step toward healing the soul. It is a choice to live with an open heart, to embrace the present with grace, and to step into the future with hope. The inner work of forgiveness challenges you to rise above the pain, to find meaning in the hurt, and to transform suffering into wisdom. In doing so, you not only heal your own soul but contribute to the healing of the world around you, spreading ripples of compassion and understanding that can bridge divides and mend hearts.

"Forgiveness as the Pathway: Healing the Mind the Body the Soul"

Soulful practices to embrace forgiveness

Embracing forgiveness on a soulful level involves engaging in practices that nurture deep, internal shifts—transcending mere cognitive understanding to touch the essence of your being. These practices facilitate a connection with the most profound aspects of ourselves and the universe, guiding us toward a state of forgiveness that heals the soul and fosters spiritual growth. Here are several soulful practices designed to support this transformative journey:

- **Meditation and Mindful Reflection:** Meditation provides a quiet space to explore the inner self, offering clarity and calm that can pave the way for forgiveness. Mindful reflection allows you to observe your thoughts and emotions without judgment, understanding their origins and their hold over you. Loving-kindness meditation, in particular, cultivates feelings of compassion towards yourself and others, gently eroding barriers to forgiveness.

- **Spiritual Dialogue:** Spiritual dialogue, regardless of one's religious beliefs, can be a powerful conduit for expressing desire for forgiveness and seeking strength to forgive. It is a personal dialogue with the divine or the universe, asking for guidance, clarity, and the capacity to forgive. This practice can provide comfort, support, and a sense of connection to something greater than oneself, reinforcing the spiritual dimensions of forgiveness.

- **Rituals and Ceremonies:** Creating personal or communal rituals can be a meaningful way to symbolize the act of forgiveness. These might include writing down grievances and then burning the paper as a symbol of release, or participating in traditional ceremonies that focus on reconciliation and forgiveness. Such rituals can provide a tangible sense of closure and a concrete step towards healing.

- **Acts of Kindness and Service:** Engaging in acts of kindness or volunteer service can shift your focus from inward pain to outward giving, fostering empathy and compassion. Helping others can be a powerful reminder of the interconnectedness of all lives, encouraging a broader perspective that makes forgiveness more accessible.

- **Expressive Arts:** The arts offer a unique pathway to explore and express feelings related to forgiveness. Painting, writing, music, and dance can all serve as outlets for emotions, helping to process feelings of hurt and anger. These creative expressions can unlock deeper understanding and empathy, both for oneself and for those who have caused pain.

"Forgiveness as the Pathway: Healing the Mind the Body the Soul"

> **Nature Connection:** Spending time in nature can be a profound practice for embracing forgiveness. The natural world, with its cycles of growth, decay, and renewal, mirrors the process of healing and forgiveness, reminding you of the continuity of life and the possibility of new beginnings. Nature's inherent beauty and tranquility can also soothe the soul, creating a conducive environment for forgiveness to blossom.
> **Yoga and Body Movement:** Yoga and other forms of body movement integrate physical postures with breath control and meditation, promoting harmony between body, mind, and spirit. These practices can help release physical manifestations of emotional pain, facilitating a state of balance and openness needed for forgiveness.
> **Community and Shared Healing:** Participating in a community that supports forgiveness and healing can amplify your efforts and provide a sense of belonging and understanding. Sharing experiences with others who are on similar paths can offer insights, encouragement, and a collective energy that nurtures forgiveness.

These soulful practices provide a holistic approach to embracing forgiveness, one that nurtures the mind, body, and spirit. By integrating these practices into your life, you embark on a journey of deep healing that transcends the act of forgiving, leading to profound personal transformation and spiritual renewal.

As we draw the curtains on Chapter 6, we stand at the threshold of a newfound understanding, basking in the gentle light of wisdom that forgiveness bestows upon the soul. This exploration into the spiritual journey of forgiveness has revealed it as not merely an act of benevolence towards those who have wronged us but as a profound pilgrimage towards inner peace, soulful healing, and spiritual awakening. Through the intricate tapestry of thoughts, emotions, and reflections you have navigated, it becomes evident that forgiveness is the key that unlocks the deepest chambers of your being, allowing light to heal the shadows that have long resided within.

Embarking on this journey demands courage to confront your deepest wounds, wisdom to understand the multifaceted nature of human frailty, and compassion to extend grace not only to others but, importantly, to yourself. It is a path that challenges you to rise above the pain, to see beyond the immediacy of hurt, towards a horizon where peace and understanding reign supreme. In healing the soul, forgiveness liberates you from the chains of resentment, setting you free to experience the richness of life with hearts unburdened by the past.

"Forgiveness as the Pathway: Healing the Mind the Body the Soul"

The practices and insights shared within these pages serve as beacons along this journey, guiding you towards embracing forgiveness in its most genuine form. They remind you that forgiveness is not a momentary lapse of memory but a deliberate choice to live with an open heart, to weave compassion into the fabric of your daily lives, and to view every encounter as an opportunity for grace and understanding.

As you conclude this chapter, let you carry forward the message that to forgive is to embark on the highest form of spiritual journey—one that leads you back to the essence of your true self. It is a journey that transcends the confines of time and space, connecting you to the eternal truth that in forgiveness, you find the purest expression of love and humanity. This journey does not promise to be easy, but it is one rich with the promise of transformation, offering a pathway to a soul healed by the gentle power of forgiveness, radiant with the light of inner peace and spiritual renewal.

7 LIVING A LIFE OF FORGIVENESS

"Living a life of forgiveness is like walking through the world with a lantern in your hand, casting light on shadows of the past, illuminating paths of peace, and guiding the soul towards boundless grace and understanding."

Embarking on a life of forgiveness is to choose a path less traveled, one that weaves through the terrains of the heart with the purpose of transforming every encounter into a lesson of compassion, understanding, and peace. This journey does not suggest a life untouched by hurt or betrayal, but rather a life that approaches such inevitable human experiences with a profound wisdom and grace. Living a life of forgiveness is about cultivating an enduring spirit of benevolence, a steadfast resolve that chooses healing over resentment, love over anger, and unity over division.

To live a life of forgiveness is to recognize that forgiveness is not a one-time act but a continuous practice—a daily choice that colors your perceptions, guides your actions, and shapes your interactions with the world. It is about nurturing an internal environment where forgiveness thrives, supported by habits, attitudes, and beliefs that foster emotional generosity and resilience. This way of living does not merely react to instances of hurt but proactively incorporates forgiveness into the very fabric of one's being, making it a cornerstone of one's ethos.

In this chapter, you delve into the transformative power of adopting forgiveness as a way of life. It is a commitment that extends beyond the personal sphere, influencing communities and societies by exemplifying the strength and beauty of forgiveness.

Living a life of forgiveness challenges you to rise above the cycle of hurt and retribution, to see the humanity in everyone, including those who have caused pain. It invites you to break down the walls built by grievances, to open your heart to empathy, and to mend bridges once thought irreparable. This journey is marked by moments of profound vulnerability and incredible strength, as you learn to release the burden of grudges and embrace the freedom and lightness that come with genuine forgiveness.

"Forgiveness as the Pathway: Healing the Mind the Body the Soul"

Moreover, a life of forgiveness enriches your soul, offering a perspective that sees beyond the immediate pain to the potential for growth, connection, and deeper understanding. It is a life that acknowledges the complexity of human emotions and relationships, choosing to respond with a compassion that heals and uplifts. As you incorporate forgiveness into the fabric of your daily existence, you not only transform your own life but also touch the lives of others, spreading ripples of kindness and healing that can change the world.

This chapter serves as a guide and inspiration for cultivating a life rich in forgiveness, illustrating how such a life is not only possible but profoundly rewarding. It beckons you to embark on this noble journey, promising a path filled with growth, healing, and a deeper connection to the essence of who you are and who you aspire to be.

Forgiveness as a daily practice
Forgiveness as a daily practice is an intentional commitment to living with an open heart, nurturing a mindset that embraces understanding, compassion, and letting go of grievances as part of your everyday routine. This practice is not about overlooking wrongs or condoning harmful behavior but about cultivating a personal ethos that prioritizes peace, healing, and emotional freedom over resentment and anger. By integrating forgiveness into your daily life, you foster a resilient spirit capable of navigating life's challenges with grace and wisdom.

- **Starting with Self-reflection:** Begin each day with a moment of self-reflection. This could be a brief meditation, journaling session, or quiet contemplation where you consider any feelings of hurt or resentment you might be holding onto. Use this time to acknowledge these feelings without judgment, understanding them as part of your human experience.
- **Setting Intentions:** Set intentions for your day that align with the practice of forgiveness. This might involve deciding to approach interactions with an open mind, to give others the benefit of the doubt, or to consciously release any minor irritations that arise. By setting these intentions, you prime your mind to choose forgiveness in moments of conflict or misunderstanding.
- **Practicing Mindfulness:** Mindfulness throughout the day can help you become more aware of your emotional responses and the moments that may require forgiveness. When you notice feelings of annoyance, anger, or hurt creeping in, use mindfulness techniques to observe these emotions without becoming attached to them. This awareness gives you the choice to respond with forgiveness rather than react from a place of hurt.

"Forgiveness as the Pathway: Healing the Mind the Body the Soul"

- **Expressing Appreciation:** Appreciation and forgiveness are deeply interconnected. By focusing on the aspects of your life for which you are thankful, you can shift your perspective away from victimhood and resentment towards one of appreciation and abundance. Make it a daily practice to list or mentally acknowledge things you are appreciative of, enhancing your capacity to forgive.
- **Offering Forgiveness:** Actively look for opportunities to forgive throughout your day. This could be as simple as forgiving someone who cuts in front of you in traffic or choosing to let go of a minor disagreement. Each act of forgiveness, no matter how small, strengthens your forgiveness muscle, making it easier to forgive in more challenging situations.
- **Seeking Forgiveness:** Just as important as offering forgiveness is the willingness to seek it. Recognize moments when you may have caused hurt or offense, intentionally or not, and take steps to apologize and make amends. This practice of seeking forgiveness nurtures humility and empathy, essential qualities for a forgiving heart.
- **Ending the Day with Release:** Conclude your day with a ritual of release, reflecting on any moments where you struggled to forgive and consciously deciding to let them go. This might involve visualizing those grievances floating away or being washed clean, reaffirming your commitment to live a life marked by forgiveness.

Making forgiveness a daily practice is a journey towards cultivating a life filled with more peace, joy, and connectedness. It is a commitment to healing not just your own heart but also contributing to the healing of those around you, one act of forgiveness at a time. This practice transforms not only how you navigate the world but also how you perceive and interact with others, opening doors to deeper understanding, compassion, and love.

"Forgiveness as the Pathway: Healing the Mind the Body the Soul"

Nurturing relationships through forgiveness

Nurturing relationships through forgiveness is a profound approach to deepening connections and fostering a nurturing environment for growth, understanding, and lasting bonds. At the core of every relationship are the inevitable human errors—misunderstandings, mistakes, and missteps—that, if left unresolved, can create rifts and harbored resentments. Forgiveness, in this context, becomes a vital tool, not just for healing these wounds, but for turning them into opportunities for strengthening the ties that bind you to others.

Recognizing the Role of Vulnerability

Vulnerability is the cornerstone of nurturing relationships through forgiveness. It involves opening up about your feelings of hurt without placing blame, allowing both parties to see each other's perspectives more clearly. This openness paves the way for genuine understanding and empathy, setting the stage for meaningful forgiveness. By being vulnerable, you invite similar honesty and openness from others, creating a cycle of trust and intimacy that fortifies relationships.

Communicating with Compassion

Effective communication is essential when nurturing relationships through forgiveness. It involves expressing your feelings and needs in a way that is respectful and non-accusatory, focusing on "I" statements rather than "you" statements to avoid placing blame. This compassionate communication fosters a safe space for both parties to express their perspectives and feelings, making forgiveness a mutual journey towards healing and understanding.

Practicing Empathy

Empathy is the ability to understand and share the feelings of another, and it plays a critical role in forgiveness. By striving to see the situation from the other person's viewpoint, you can gain insights into their actions or words, often finding that their intentions were not to cause harm. This understanding can soften your feelings of hurt, making it easier to forgive and move forward together.

"Forgiveness as the Pathway: Healing the Mind the Body the Soul"

Choosing Forgiveness Actively
Forgiveness in relationships is a choice that must be made actively and consciously. It is deciding to let go of grudges and resentments for the sake of the relationship and your well-being. This choice does not negate the validity of your feelings but recognizes that the relationship's value outweighs the pain of past conflicts. By choosing forgiveness, you prioritize growth, healing, and the potential for joy in your connections with others.

Setting Boundaries
Forgiveness does not mean allowing yourself to be hurt repeatedly. Part of nurturing relationships through forgiveness involves setting healthy boundaries that protect your emotional well-being. These boundaries communicate to others how you wish to be treated, creating a framework within which forgiveness can occur without resentment. Healthy boundaries ensure that forgiveness becomes a step towards more respectful and mindful interactions.

Fostering a Forgiving Environment
Creating an environment where forgiveness is valued and practiced regularly can transform the dynamics of your relationships. This involves acknowledging mistakes openly, expressing apologies sincerely, and showing appreciation for each other's willingness to forgive. Such an environment encourages continuous personal and relational growth, making forgiveness a shared value that deepens trust and affection.

Letting Forgiveness Lead to Growth
Nurturing relationships through forgiveness allows every conflict or misunderstanding to become a stepping stone for growth. It offers lessons in compassion, understanding, and resilience, teaching both parties how to navigate challenges more effectively in the future. This approach turns potential divisions into sources of strength, enhancing the relationship's depth and meaning.

By integrating forgiveness into the fabric of your relationships, you cultivate a garden where trust, love, and mutual respect can flourish. This nurturing through forgiveness not only heals wounds but also enriches your connections with others, creating bonds that are resilient, deep, and profoundly fulfilling.

"Forgiveness as the Pathway: Healing the Mind the Body the Soul"

Embracing Forgiveness as a Gateway to Joy and Fulfillment
Another vital point to explore is how embracing forgiveness opens the doors to experiencing deeper joy and fulfillment in life. This section delves into the transformative power of forgiveness to not only heal past wounds but also to enhance your capacity for happiness, contentment, and a profound sense of well-being. It focuses on the positive ripple effects that forgiveness can have on your emotional landscape, enriching your experiences and interactions with the world.

Forgiveness, when truly embraced, acts as a catalyst for joy. It liberates you from the burdens of past grievances, allowing more space in your heart for positive emotions. This liberation from the chains of unforgiveness means no longer being anchored to negative past experiences. Instead, you find yourself more present, more open to the beauty and joy in the moment, and more capable of cultivating happiness in your life.

Strategies for Embracing Forgiveness to Enhance Joy and Fulfillment
- **Mindful Celebration of the Present:** Engage in practices that ground you in the present moment, appreciating the beauty and abundance around you. This could involve mindfulness exercises, spending time in nature, or simply savoring the small pleasures of daily life.
- **Positive Relationship Building:** Actively seek to build and nurture relationships based on mutual respect, understanding, and forgiveness. Positive social connections are foundational to experiencing joy and fulfillment.
- **Pursuit of Passion and Purpose:** Use the energy and freedom gained from forgiveness to pursue activities and goals that bring you joy and a sense of purpose. Engaging in meaningful work or hobbies can significantly enhance your sense of fulfillment.
- **Appreciation Practice:** Cultivate a daily practice of appreciation, focusing on the aspects of your life that bring you joy and satisfaction. This practice can shift your focus from what is lacking to the abundance that exists in your life.
- **Acts of Kindness:** Regularly engage in acts of kindness, both big and small. Giving to others without expectation of return can create a profound sense of joy and connection, reinforcing the positive aspects of forgiveness.
- **Personal Growth and Learning:** View every experience, including those that require forgiveness, as an opportunity for personal growth and learning. Adopting a growth mindset can transform challenges into opportunities for joy and discovery.

"Forgiveness as the Pathway: Healing the Mind the Body the Soul"

By integrating forgiveness into the very essence of how you live, you not only heal from past pains but also open yourself to a life marked by greater joy and fulfillment. You have explored the nuanced ways in which forgiveness enriches your daily life, offering practical insights and strategies for those seeking to deepen their capacity for happiness. Through reflections and guidance illuminate the path to a life where forgiveness and joy are intertwined, showing how letting go of past hurts can unveil a more vibrant, fulfilling existence.

As you draw Chapter 7 to a close, it is clear that living a life of forgiveness is not merely an ideal to aspire to, but a tangible, daily practice that enriches your life and the lives of those around us. This journey of continual forgiveness challenges you to transcend your immediate reactions of hurt and resentment, inviting you into a deeper exploration of compassion, understanding, and genuine peace. Living a life of forgiveness is an act of profound courage and love—a testament to the strength of the human spirit and its capacity to heal, grow, and transform even in the face of deep wounds.

Through the insights and practices shared in this chapter, you have been equipped with the tools to integrate forgiveness into the fabric of your daily life, transforming routine interactions into opportunities for healing and connection. This way of living asks you to remain open to the complexities of human relationships, to navigate the nuances of hurt and healing with grace, and to choose forgiveness, even when it seems counterintuitive.

The path to living a life of forgiveness is marked by moments of profound vulnerability and incredible strength. It is a journey that does not shy away from the pain or the complexity of human emotions but instead faces them with a heart willing to understand and forgive. This commitment to forgiveness not only heals the wounds of the past but also opens up new possibilities for love, joy, and deep, meaningful connections.

Moreover, as you embrace forgiveness as a way of life, you become a beacon of peace and understanding in a world that sorely needs it. Your decision to forgive—repeatedly and generously—can inspire others to embark on their own journeys of healing, creating ripples of compassion and transformation that extend far beyond your immediate circle. In this way, living a life of forgiveness contributes to the healing of the collective human spirit, fostering a more compassionate, empathetic, and understanding world.

"Forgiveness as the Pathway: Healing the Mind the Body the Soul"

In conclusion, living a life of forgiveness is an ongoing journey of self-discovery, healing, and growth. It is a powerful choice that not only liberates you from the chains of bitterness and resentment but also enriches your relationships and the world around you. As you move forward, let the principles and practices of forgiveness guide you, nurturing a life filled with greater peace, love, and fulfillment. May your commitment to living a life of forgiveness illuminate your path and touch the lives of all you encounter, fostering a legacy of healing and hope for generations to come.

8 TOOLS AND EXERCISES FOR FORGIVENESS

"Forgiveness is like a tapestry woven with threads of courage, understanding, and compassion. Through tools and exercises, we can craft this tapestry, creating a masterpiece of peace and liberation within our hearts."

Embarking on the journey of forgiveness requires more than just a willing heart; it necessitates practical tools and exercises that guides you through the often complex and challenging process of letting go of resentment, understanding pain, and opening your heart to compassion and healing. This chapter serves as a toolbox for those ready to embrace forgiveness, offering a collection of carefully curated practices designed to facilitate emotional release, foster empathy, and cultivate a lasting sense of peace.

Forgiveness, while deeply personal, follows certain universal principles that can be navigated with the help of specific strategies and techniques. These tools and exercises are not one-size-fits-all solutions but rather a palette from which you can choose what resonates most deeply with your unique journey towards forgiveness. From reflective writing prompts and guided meditations to expressive arts and communication techniques, each tool serves a purpose in unraveling the layers of hurt, bitterness, and misunderstanding that obstruct the path to forgiveness.

This chapter delves into the heart of forgiveness practice, breaking down the process into manageable steps and providing clear, actionable exercises that you can integrate into your daily life. Whether you are seeking to forgive yourself, another person, or even circumstances beyond control, these tools are designed to meet you where you are, offering support, guidance, and clarity as you navigate the emotional landscape of forgiveness.

The exercises outlined here are grounded in psychological research, spiritual wisdom, and real-world applicability, ensuring that they are not only effective but deeply transformative. They aim to shift your perspective, challenge your preconceptions, and ultimately lead you to a place of genuine forgiveness and healing. Along the way, you will be invited to explore the depths of your emotions, to confront and release past pains, and to rediscover the power of compassion and empathy—both for yourself and for others.

As you journey through this chapter, approach each tool and exercise with

"Forgiveness as the Pathway: Healing the Mind the Body the Soul"

an open mind and a gentle heart, remembering that forgiveness is a process that unfolds in its own time. These practices are your companions on the path to forgiveness, offering light and guidance as you weave your own tapestry of healing and liberation. By actively engaging with these tools and exercises, you will not only navigate the intricacies of forgiveness but also embark on a profound journey of personal growth and renewal, paving the way for a life filled with more peace, joy, and fulfillment.

Mindfulness and meditation
Mindfulness and meditation stand as foundational practices in the journey of forgiveness, offering a path to inner peace by helping you cultivate awareness, presence, and compassion. These practices serve as powerful tools for navigating the emotional complexities of forgiveness, allowing you to observe your thoughts and feelings without judgment and to understand the deep roots of your reactions. By integrating mindfulness and meditation into your forgiveness process, you engage in a transformative experience that not only facilitates letting go of resentment but also promotes healing and emotional freedom.

Mindfulness: The Art of Presence
Mindfulness involves maintaining a moment-by-moment awareness of your thoughts, feelings, bodily sensations, and the surrounding environment with openness and curiosity. It teaches you to observe your experiences without getting caught up in them, providing a space to recognize and accept your feelings of hurt or anger. This awareness is crucial in the forgiveness process, as it allows you to identify the pain points that need healing and to approach them with kindness rather than avoidance or reactivity.

Practicing mindfulness can begin with simple exercises such as focusing on your breath, engaging in mindful walking, or performing daily tasks with full attention. These practices help anchor you in the present moment, reducing the tendency to ruminate on past grievances or worry about future implications. As you become more present, you are able to see the situation that requires forgiveness more clearly, without the distortion of overwhelming emotions.

Meditation: Cultivating Compassion and Empathy
Meditation, particularly practices like loving-kindness (Metta) meditation, directly supports the forgiveness process by cultivating feelings of compassion and empathy towards yourself and others. This form of meditation involves silently repeating phrases of goodwill and kindness towards yourself, a loved one, a neutral person, someone you have difficulty with, and finally, all beings. Through this practice, you gently dissolve the

"Forgiveness as the Pathway: Healing the Mind the Body the Soul"

barriers of resentment, opening your heart to a deeper understanding of the interconnectedness of all people.
Loving-kindness meditation nurtures a compassionate response to pain and suffering—yours and that of others. It softens the heart, making it easier to forgive by recognizing that everyone, including those who have wronged you, seeks happiness and suffers in their way. This shared human experience becomes a common ground for forgiveness, fostering a sense of empathy that transcends personal grievances.

Integrating Mindfulness and Meditation into Daily Life
To effectively use mindfulness and meditation in the forgiveness process, consistency is key. Setting aside regular times for practice can create a routine that nurtures your capacity for forgiveness. Additionally, incorporating mindfulness into daily activities—such as eating, walking, or even during difficult conversations—can help maintain a balanced perspective, especially in moments when forgiveness feels most challenging.

Mindfulness and meditation are not quick fixes but deeply transformative practices that require patience and dedication. Over time, they can significantly alter how you relate to yourself and others, promoting a life characterized by deeper peace, resilience, and openness to forgiveness. Through these practices, you learn to release the hold of past hurts, to live with greater presence and compassion, and to embrace the healing power of forgiveness in your journey toward wholeness and well-being.

Mindfulness Exercise: The Five Senses Exercise

This mindfulness exercise is designed to ground you in the present moment, helping reduce stress and enhance your awareness, which can be particularly beneficial when navigating feelings of hurt or resentment.

- **Find a Comfortable Spot:** Sit or stand in a place where you can remain undisturbed for a few minutes.
- **Notice Five Things You Can See:** Look around you and mentally note five things that you can see. Pick something that you don't normally notice, like a shadow or a small crack in the concrete.
- **Acknowledge Four Things You Can Touch:** Feel the texture of four objects around you. This could be the fabric of your clothes, the smooth surface of a table, or the grass under your feet.
- **Identify Three Things You Can Hear:** Close your eyes and tune into three sounds. Listen for subtle noises you might typically overlook, such as the hum of a refrigerator or distant bird chirps.
- **Recognize Two Things You Can Smell:** Acknowledge two things that you can smell. If you are indoors, this might be harder, so you might choose to walk near a window or smell your own skin or clothes.
- **Notice One Thing You Can Taste:** Focus on one thing that you can taste at this moment. It can be the aftertaste of a meal, a sip of a drink, or even the taste of your own mouth.

This exercise brings you into the present, helping shift your focus away from ruminating on past events or future worries, creating a space where forgiveness can begin to take root.

"Forgiveness as the Pathway: Healing the Mind the Body the Soul"

Meditation Exercise: Loving-Kindness Meditation (Metta)
Loving-kindness meditation fosters feelings of compassion and love towards yourself and others, which is essential for healing and forgiveness.
- **Find a Quiet Space:** Sit in a comfortable position in a place where you will not be disturbed. Close your eyes and take a few deep breaths to relax.
- **Generate Warm Feelings:** Begin by thinking of someone who makes you feel happy and loved. Visualize their face and feel the warmth and love emanating from them towards you.
- **Direct Loving-Kindness to Yourself:** Silently repeat phrases of loving-kindness towards yourself, such as "May I be happy. May I be healthy. May I be safe. May I live with ease."
- **Expand Your Circle:** Gradually extend these feelings of loving-kindness to others. Start with someone you feel warmly towards, then someone neutral, followed by someone with whom you have difficulty, and finally, to all beings everywhere. Use the same phrases, adjusting them as needed (e.g., "May you be happy. May you be healthy.").
- **Feel the Connection:** As you send these wishes of loving-kindness out, imagine a gentle wave of compassion and love flowing from your heart to others, connecting you with the universal desire for happiness and peace.
- **Conclude with Appreciation:** Finish your meditation by taking a few deep breaths and feeling appreciative for the opportunity to connect with these feelings of loving-kindness. Open your eyes when you are ready.

Practicing this meditation regularly can help soften feelings of anger and bitterness, opening the path to forgiveness and healing interpersonal wounds.

"Forgiveness as the Pathway: Healing the Mind the Body the Soul"

Journaling and reflective practices
Journaling and reflective practices offer powerful avenues for exploring the depths of your emotions, understanding the roots of your forgiveness journey, and facilitating personal growth and healing. By putting pen to paper, you engage in a dialogue with yourself that can reveal insights, release pent-up feelings, and clarify your thoughts and intentions regarding forgiveness. These practices are not just about recording daily events but about delving into the complexities of your inner life, offering a structured way to navigate the often turbulent waters of forgiveness.

Journaling as a Tool for Forgiveness
Journaling for forgiveness involves more than merely recounting grievances; it is an introspective process that encourages you to explore and express your deepest feelings about a situation or individual. This can include writing letters of forgiveness that you may never send, which can be particularly cathartic. Such letters allow you to articulate your feelings of hurt, your wishes for the other person's well-being, and your intentions to let go of the resentment that burdens you.

Another powerful journaling exercise is writing from the perspective of the person who hurt you. While challenging, this can foster empathy and a deeper understanding of the situation, helping break down barriers to forgiveness. Additionally, appreciation journaling can shift your focus from pain to appreciation, highlighting positive aspects of your life and relationships that forgiveness can enhance.

Reflective Practices to Deepen Understanding
Reflective practices complement journaling by providing a broader framework for contemplation and insight. This can include meditation on forgiveness, where you reflect on the nature of forgiveness, its importance in your life, and the barriers you face in forgiving. Visualization exercises can also be powerful, where you imagine the act of forgiving someone or receiving forgiveness, experiencing the emotional release and peace that follows.

Mindful walking or other mindfulness exercises focused on forgiveness can help integrate forgiveness into your daily life, making it a living practice rather than an abstract concept. During these activities, you can reflect on forgiveness, allowing insights to arise naturally as you engage in the physical act of moving forward, symbolizing your journey towards healing and liberation.

"Forgiveness as the Pathway: Healing the Mind the Body the Soul"

The Benefits of Journaling and Reflective Practices

The benefits of journaling and reflective practices in the context of forgiveness are manifold. They provide a safe, private space to confront and process emotions, leading to significant stress reduction and emotional clarity. These practices can also break the cycle of rumination, shifting your focus from past hurts to present healing and future growth.

Moreover, journaling and reflection promote self-awareness, helping you understand your role in conflicts and how your thoughts and actions contribute to your well-being. This can lead to greater emotional intelligence, empathy, and compassion, both for yourself and others. Over time, engaging in these practices can transform how you perceive forgiveness, turning it from a difficult obligation into a liberating choice that nurtures your soul.

In sum, journaling and reflective practices are invaluable tools in the forgiveness process, offering pathways to explore the depths of your emotions, understand your experiences, and ultimately, find peace and closure. Through regular engagement with these practices, you can cultivate a deeper sense of self-awareness and embark on a transformative journey of healing, growth, and renewal.

"Forgiveness as the Pathway: Healing the Mind the Body the Soul"

Journaling Exercise: The Forgiveness Letter

This exercise involves writing a letter of forgiveness, either to someone who has wronged you or to yourself, as a way to articulate and process feelings of hurt, anger, and ultimately, release.

- **Set the Scene:** Choose a quiet and comfortable space where you feel safe and undisturbed. Have your journal or a piece of paper and a pen ready.
- **Start with Reflection:** Before you begin writing, take a few moments to reflect on the situation or the person you wish to forgive. Acknowledge the emotions that arise, allowing yourself to feel them fully.
- **Write the Letter:** Begin your letter by clearly stating whom you are forgiving and what you are forgiving them for. Describe how their actions affected you, expressing all the emotions you have felt without holding back.
- **Express Understanding:** If possible, try to empathize with the person you are writing to. This does not mean excusing their behavior, but perhaps acknowledging any circumstances or challenges they were facing at the time.
- **Declare Forgiveness:** Clearly state your intention to forgive. This might be challenging, but remember, forgiveness is a gift you give yourself. It is about freeing yourself from the burden of resentment.
- **Reflect on Growth:** End the letter by reflecting on what you have learned from the experience and how it has contributed to your growth. Affirm your decision to move forward, free from the weight of past hurt.
- **Closure:** You don not need to send the letter. Some people find it helpful to keep it in a safe place, while others prefer a symbolic gesture of letting go, such as tearing it up or safely burning it.

"Forgiveness as the Pathway: Healing the Mind the Body the Soul"

Reflective Practice: The Forgiveness Meditation
This guided reflection helps you visualize the process of forgiving, allowing you to emotionally and mentally work through feelings of hurt and release.

- **Find a Quiet Space:** Sit or lie down in a comfortable position in a quiet space where you will not be interrupted. Close your eyes and take several deep breaths to center yourself.
- **Visualize the Person or Situation:** Bring to mind the person or situation you wish to forgive. Try to picture it/him/her as clearly as possible.
- **Acknowledge Your Feelings:** Recognize and name the emotions you are feeling. Allow yourself to feel them without judgment. Acknowledge the impact this situation or person has had on your life.
- **Extend Compassion:** Imagine sending compassionate thoughts to yourself and the person you are forgiving. You might visualize a healing light enveloping you both or simply wish for peace and happiness for yourself and them.
- **Speak Forgiveness:** Silently or aloud, express your forgiveness. You might say something like, "I forgive you, and I release you. I wish you well. I choose to let go and move forward with peace."
- **Reflect on Release:** Take a moment to feel the weight lifting off your shoulders. Visualize yourself moving forward, lighter and at peace.
- **Conclude with Appreciation:** End the meditation by focusing on something you are appreciative of. This could be your strength to forgive, a lesson learned, or the growth you have experienced.

"Forgiveness as the Pathway: Healing the Mind the Body the Soul"

Forgiveness rituals and ceremonies
Forgiveness rituals and ceremonies harness the symbolic power of actions and intentions to facilitate the process of letting go of resentment and embracing healing and renewal. These rituals, whether personal or communal, provide a structured and meaningful way to externalize inner feelings of forgiveness, marking significant steps on the journey towards emotional liberation. Here is a deeper exploration into the significance and variety of forgiveness rituals and ceremonies:

> **Creating a Personal Forgiveness Ritual:** A personal forgiveness ritual can be a powerful way to signify your commitment to forgiving someone, including yourself. This might involve setting aside a specific time and space to engage in acts that symbolize letting go and moving forward. For instance, you could write down the grievances or names of those you wish to forgive on pieces of paper and then release them into a body of water, bury them, or safely burn them, symbolizing the release of those burdens from your life. The act of physically letting go helps to reinforce your emotional intention to forgive.

> **Lighting Candles for Forgiveness:** Lighting candles as a forgiveness ritual can be a serene and hopeful act. You might choose a candle to represent each person you are forgiving (or seeking forgiveness from) and one for yourself, symbolizing self-forgiveness. As you light each candle, spend a moment reflecting on the hurt and your wish for healing and peace for both you and the other person. The act of lighting the candle signifies your willingness to bring light to the shadowed parts of your heart, illuminating a path to reconciliation and understanding.

> **Planting a Forgiveness Garden:** Gardening is a ritual that symbolizes growth, renewal, and the cycle of life—making it a potent metaphor for forgiveness. You can create a forgiveness garden by planting flowers or trees that represent your journey towards forgiveness. Each plant can symbolize a particular aspect of forgiveness you are working on or a person you are forgiving. As you tend the garden, you nurture not only the plants but also your capacity for forgiveness, watching both grow and flourish over time.

"Forgiveness as the Pathway: Healing the Mind the Body the Soul"

- **Forgiveness Walks:** Forgiveness walks can be a meditative and symbolic journey. As you walk, reflect on the steps needed to forgive and imagine each step as a move away from resentment and towards peace. This can be particularly powerful in a natural setting, where the surroundings echo the themes of renewal and beauty arising from letting go.
- **Using Water in Forgiveness Rituals:** Water is often associated with cleansing and renewal. A forgiveness ritual involving water might include writing down hurts on soluble paper and dissolving them in water, symbolizing the washing away of grievances. Alternatively, standing in a body of water and releasing stones or petals while focusing on forgiveness intentions can be a powerful act of emotional and symbolic release.
- **Forgiveness and Release Ceremonies with Objects:** This involves choosing an object that represents the pain or resentment you are holding onto—such as a rock for its weight—and then choosing a meaningful way to dispose of it, such as throwing it into the sea or a deep lake. The physical act of throwing away the object symbolizes discarding the emotional weight you have been carrying.

These rituals and ceremonies provide a tangible way to process and express forgiveness, turning internal intentions into external actions. By engaging in these practices, you create meaningful moments that mark your journey towards healing, offering not only personal liberation but also the potential to transform relationships and communities with the power of forgiveness.

"Forgiveness as the Pathway: Healing the Mind the Body the Soul"

As you reach the conclusion of "Forgiveness as the Pathway: Healing Mind, Body, and Soul," you stand at the precipice of a profound understanding: that forgiveness is not merely an act of letting go but a transformative journey that heals you to your very core. Throughout this exploration, you have delved into the multifaceted nature of forgiveness, uncovering its power to mend the fractures within your mind, soothe the ailments of your bodies, and restore the harmony of your soul.

Forgiveness, as you have seen, is an intricate dance between strength and vulnerability, a balance between acknowledging your pain and choosing to rise above it. It challenges you to face your deepest wounds, not with resentment, but with compassion and understanding. This journey, while personal, resonates with the universal human experience of seeking peace, connection, and liberation from the chains of past hurts.

Through exercises, rituals and reflective practices, you equipped yourself with the means to navigate the complexities of forgiveness. These practices are not mere steps but lanterns lighting your path, guiding you through the darkness of resentment towards the light of understanding and peace. They remind you that forgiveness is a choice—a choice to heal, to grow, and to love more deeply.

Living a life of forgiveness is perhaps the most profound commitment you can make—not only to yourself but to the world around you. It is a declaration that you choose healing over harm, unity over division, and love over all else. As you integrate forgiveness into the fabric of your daily life, you not only transform your own heart but also contribute to the healing of your communities and the world at large.

In embracing forgiveness, you discover that it is indeed the pathway to healing mind, body, and soul. It is the key to unlocking your fullest potential for joy, peace, and fulfillment. As you move forward on this journey, let you carry the lessons of forgiveness with you, allowing them to shape your interactions, inform your choices, and guide your steps. May you approach each day with a forgiving heart, open to the possibilities of new beginnings and the promise of a life renewed.

"Forgiveness as the Pathway: Healing Mind, Body, and Soul" is a call to action—a call to embrace the transformative power of forgiveness, to embark on this sacred journey of healing, and to discover the boundless grace that lies in the act of letting go. As you close this chapter, may you open another, stepping into a future where forgiveness is your compass, leading you to a place where peace and wholeness reign supreme.

"Forgiveness as the Pathway: Healing the Mind the Body the Soul"

STORIES OF FORGIVENESS

Anna's Journey to Self-Forgiveness
Anna's life was overshadowed by a grave mistake she made in her early twenties, leading to a strained relationship with her family and the loss of close friendships. For years, she carried the weight of guilt and self-loathing, which manifested in chronic anxiety and depression. Her healing journey began when she decided to seek therapy, where she learned the importance of self-compassion and the power of self-forgiveness.

Through journaling and mindfulness practices, Anna confronted her past actions, acknowledging the hurt she caused and understanding the circumstances that led to those choices. She learned to view herself with compassion rather than judgment, recognizing that her mistake did not define her worth. Over time, Anna's practice of self-forgiveness allowed her to rebuild her self-esteem and mend the relationships that were damaged. Forgiving herself was the key that unlocked a life of peace, allowing her to move forward with hope and a renewed sense of purpose. Anna's story highlights the profound impact of self-forgiveness on healing and personal growth.

Michael's Reconciliation with His Father
Michael grew up harboring resentment towards his father for his absence and neglect during his childhood. This unresolved anger affected Michael's relationships and his overall well-being, leading to bouts of anger and a pervasive sense of unhappiness. The turning point came when Michael became a father himself and faced the challenges of parenthood firsthand.

Motivated by a desire to break the cycle of estrangement, Michael reached out to his father, initiating a series of difficult but honest conversations. Through these dialogues, Michael came to understand the struggles his father had faced, including his own feelings of inadequacy and regret. Michael's decision to forgive was not immediate but evolved through these interactions, culminating in a heartfelt reconciliation that healed years of hurt and misunderstanding.

Forgiveness allowed Michael to release the bitterness that had tainted his view of life, opening his heart to the joys of fatherhood and the possibility of a new beginning with his own father. This healing journey transformed Michael's relationships, instilling in him a deep sense of inner peace and fulfillment.

"Forgiveness as the Pathway: Healing the Mind the Body the Soul"

Layla's Path to Healing After Betrayal

Layla's trust was shattered when she discovered her long-term partner's infidelity. The betrayal plunged her into a deep depression, eroding her trust in others and her self-worth. For years, Layla was imprisoned by her inability to forgive, her pain turning into a barrier that prevented her from forming new relationships.

The journey to forgiveness began when Layla attended a retreat focused on healing and forgiveness. Through workshops that included guided meditations, group sharing, and forgiveness rituals, Layla confronted her pain and slowly began to let go of her anger. She learned to separate her partner's actions from her self-value and realized that forgiveness was essential for her healing.

Choosing to forgive her partner was a liberating experience for Layla. It did not mean reconciling with him or diminishing the hurt she felt but acknowledging her pain and deciding not to let it control her life. This act of forgiveness was transformative, allowing Layla to heal fully, regain her sense of self-worth, and open herself to love and trust again. Through forgiveness, Layla found a profound sense of peace and a renewed capacity for joy.

These stories of forgiveness illuminate the diverse paths individuals can take toward healing and the universal truth that forgiveness—whether of oneself or others—is a powerful catalyst for emotional and spiritual renewal.

"Forgiveness as the Pathway: Healing the Mind the Body the Soul"

ABOUT THE AUTHOR

At the heart of "Forgiveness as the Pathway: Healing Mind, Body, and Soul" is a 51-year-old divine being whose own journey of forgiveness—from the shadows of childhood to the light of adulthood—inspired the core of this transformative guide. A pivotal conversation with a dear loved one, revealing his deep-seated pain from his past, sparked the inception of this book. It is a narrative born out of the need to demonstrate that forgiveness is not only a possibility but a powerful pathway to healing and liberation.

Through my own practices and exercises of forgiveness, I have navigated the complexities of reconciling with both myself and those from my past. My journey is a testament to the resilience of the human spirit and the profound power of forgiveness. Now living a life marked by peace and a deep awareness of my inner being, I share my wisdom, experiences, and the tools that have led me to a state of profound inner peace and fulfillment.

This book intricately weaves personal anecdotes with practical guidance, offering readers a compassionate roadmap towards releasing emotional burdens and fostering physical healing and spiritual renewal. It delves into mindfulness, meditation, journaling, reflective practices, and the significance of rituals and ceremonies in the forgiveness process. It addresses the interconnectedness of mind, body, and soul in healing, emphasizing the critical role of self-forgiveness and the power of forgiveness within communities.

"Forgiveness as the Pathway: Healing Mind, Body, and Soul" stands as an invitation to you to embark on your own journeys of forgiveness. Written with the hope of guiding a dear loved one—and others like him—towards the path of forgiveness, my story is a beacon of hope and a reminder that forgiveness is within reach for all who seek it. This book is not just a guide but a heartfelt message to my loved one and to the world: that I have found the strength to forgive, and so can they.

Printed in Great Britain
by Amazon